Privacy and Data Protection Law in United Kingdom

Privacy and Data Protection Law in United Kingdom

Joseph Savirimuthu

Maria Tzanou

This book was originally published as a monograph in the International Encyclopaedia of Laws/Privacy and Technology Law.

Founding Editor: Roger Blanpain
General Editor: Frank Hendrickx
Volume Editors: Jos Dumortier, Pieter Gryffroy, Ruben Roex & Yung Shin Van Der Sype

Wolters Kluwer

Published by:
Kluwer Law International B.V.
PO Box 316
2400 AH Alphen aan den Rijn
The Netherlands
E-mail: lrs-sales@wolterskluwer.com
Website: www.wolterskluwer.com/en/solutions/kluwerlawinternational

Sold and distributed by:
Wolters Kluwer Legal & Regulatory U.S.
920 Links Avenue
Landisville, PA 17538
United States of America
E-mail: customer.service@wolterskluwer.com

ISBN 978-94-035-2236-4

e-Book: ISBN 978-94-035-2416-0
web-PDF: ISBN 978-94-035-2426-9

The Authors

Dr Joseph Savirimuthu is a Senior Lecturer in the Liverpool Law School, School of Law and Social Justice at the University of Liverpool, UK. His research examines the regulatory challenges posed by new and emerging technologies. Specifically, the research interests and publications straddle the broad domains of regulatory and governance challenges raised by new and emerging technologies, with particular focus on privacy and data protection and related ethical/moral anxieties. He is the author of *Online Child Safety: Law, Technology and Governance* (Palgrave, 2012) and is currently working on a monograph, *Thinking with Algorithms*. Joseph is a member of working groups in the IEEE (P7102), NHS AI Labs public dialogue on patient data and the editor for the *Internet Policy Review*.

Dr Maria Tzanou is a Senior Lecturer (Associate Professor) in Law at the University of Sheffield, UK. Her research focuses on European constitutional and human rights law, privacy, data protection, AI, big data, surveillance and the inequalities of data privacy law and how these affect vulnerable groups. She has published numerous journal articles and book chapters on data privacy. She is the author of *The Fundamental Right to Data Protection: Normative Value in the Context of Counter-Terrorism Surveillance* (Hart, 2017) and the editor of *Personal Data Protection and Legal Developments in the European Union* (IGI Global, 2020) and *Health Data Privacy under the GDPR. Big Data Challenges and Regulatory Responses* (Routledge, 2021). She acts as permanent scientific advisor to the Greek Ministry of Justice on data protection issues, co-convenes the UK Society of Legal Scholars (SLS) Cyberlaw Section and is an Associate Editor of *European Data Protection Law Review*.

The Authors

Table of Contents

Table of Contents

List of Abbreviations

AI	Artificial Intelligence
BCR	Binding Corporate Rules
BGI	Browse Generated Information
CLOUD	Clarifying Lawful Overseas Use of Data
CJEU	Court of Justice of the European Union
CoE	Council of Europe
DCMS	Digital, Culture Media and Sport
DPA	Data Protection Act
DPA 1998	Data Protection Act 1998
DPA 2018	Data Protection Act 2018
DPPEC	Data Protection, Privacy and Electronic Communications (Amendments etc.) (EU Exit) Regulations 2019
DPIA	Data Protection Impact Assessment
DPO	Data Protection Officer
EC	European Commission
ECHR	European Convention on Human Rights
ECtHR	European Court of Human Rights
EDPB	European Data Protection Board
EDPS	European Data Protection Supervisor
EEA	European Economic Area
EIR	Environmental Information Regulations
EU	European Union
EUWA	European Union (Withdrawal) Act
EU GDPR	European Union General Data Protection Regulation
FOI	Freedom of Information
FOIA	Freedom of Information Act
FSA	Financial Service Authority
GDPR	General Data Protection Regulation
HRA	Human Rights Act 1998
ICO	Information Commissioner's Office

List of Abbreviations

IP	Internet Protocol
LED	Law Enforcement Directive
LPP	Legal Professional Privilege
NCSC	National Cyber Security Centre
NCND	Non-Circumvention and Non-Disclosure
NHS	National Health Service
MLAT	Mutual Legal Assistance Treaty
MoU	Memorandum of Understanding
PECR	Privacy and Electronic Communications (EC Directive) Regulations 2003
SAR	Subject Access Request
UK	United Kingdom
UK GDPR	United Kingdom General Data Protection Regulation
US	United States

General Introduction

1. The data protection legal framework of the United Kingdom of Great Britain and Northern Ireland is characterised by a number of interesting elements. First, this legal framework is heavily influenced by European Union (EU) law, policy and jurisprudence as the United Kingdom (UK) has been an EU Member State for several decades before its withdrawal on 31 January 2020. Such influence is also evident in the current post-Brexit era. In particular, the current data protection legal framework in the UK is governed by three main regimes:

(1) The United Kingdom General Data Protection Regulation (UK GDPR), which constitutes the general data protection framework and implements the European Union General Data Protection Regulation (EU GDPR) in many respects.
(2) The Data Protection Act (DPA) (2018) Part 3, which regulates personal data processing for law enforcement purposes and which implements the Law Enforcement Directive (LED).
(3) The DPA Part 4, which includes the intelligence services regime.

2. Second, following Brexit, the UK has become a 'third country' from a data protection perspective. This means that personal data cannot be freely transferred from the EU to the UK absent a specific legal mechanism, in line with the requirements of the EU GDPR and the LED. In June 2021, the EU Commission adopted two decisions (one pursuant to the General Data Protection Regulation (GDPR) and one pursuant to the LED) declaring that the UK data protection regime offers an adequate level of protection, thus allowing for the transfer of personal data to the UK. However, and, third, the sustainability of the current adequacy findings is at risk when one considers the UK Government's appetite to adopt a new model for data regulation[1] that diverges significantly from EU standards until now broadly retained in UK law.

3. That being said, it should be noted that the following analysis focuses on the current UK data protection regime by discussing its different aspects. The changes that the proposed Data Reform Bill might introduce as well as their implications for the relationship between the UK and the EU are still a matter of the future and outside the scope of this contribution.

1. *See* Queen's Speech 2022 https://www.gov.uk/government/speeches/queens-speech-2022.

Part I. Privacy protection in the UK

Chapter 1. Privacy Protection in the Constitution

4. The United Kingdom is a parliamentary democracy with a constitutional sovereign as Head of State. The British people see themselves governed through their elected representatives in Parliament.[2] The UK Parliament is sovereign, this means that it is supreme to all other government institutions. The UK also has an executive accountable to the Parliament and an independent judiciary. The executive's authority derives from its ability to command the confidence of the elected House of Commons and is accountable to both Houses of Parliament (the House of Commons – the primary chamber and the House of Lords) which are responsible for scrutinising the government and debating and making laws. The UK Supreme Court, which replaced the Appellate Committee of the House of Lords as the UK's highest court in 2009, hears cases of the greatest public or constitutional importance affecting the whole UK population.

5. The United Kingdom Parliament has devolved responsibility to the Scottish Parliament, the Welsh Parliament (Senedd Cymru), and the Northern Ireland Assembly for legislating on domestic matters in Scotland, Wales and Northern Ireland which the United Kingdom Parliament has not reserved to itself. This means that there are different legal systems in the UK: there is one legal system for England and Wales, another for Scotland and a third one for Northern Ireland. For instance, criminal justice systems, including policing, of Scotland and Northern Ireland are devolved to the Scottish Parliament and Northern Ireland Assembly, respectively. The UK Supreme Court is the final Court of Appeal in the UK for civil cases, and for criminal cases from England, Wales and Northern Ireland; criminal appeals in Scotland are heard from the High Court of Justiciary in Scotland.

6. The United Kingdom does not have a codified constitution, entrenched in a single constitutive document. However, a number of constitutional principles have emerged in the UK over time, drawn from case law, conventions, statutes and treaties. These are collectively referred to as the British Constitution.

7. The protection of fundamental rights of individuals in the UK has developed over the years through the common law recognition of statutes, such as Magna

2. Colm O'Cinneide, *Human rights and the UK constitution* 7 (British Academy Policy Centre 2012).

Carta, the Bill of Rights 1689 and the Human Rights Act (HRA) 1998[3] and international treaties, in particular the European Convention on Human Rights (ECHR) which the UK ratified in 1951. Several different layers of rights protection exist in British law. First, the common law requires that public authorities must have a clear legal basis for their actions, respect the requirements of fair procedure, and act in a 'rational' manner.[4] However, the protection the common law offers against abuses of state power is mainly limited to procedural requirements.[5] Second, the HRA 1998, which incorporates the rights contained in the ECHR into the law of the United Kingdom, grants individuals the fundamental rights and freedoms provided in Articles 2 to 12 and 14 of the ECHR and Articles 1, 2 and 3 of its First Protocol and Article 1 of its Thirteenth Protocol, as read in conjunction with Articles 16, 17 and 18 of that Convention. Pursuant to the HRA, any action of public authorities must be compatible with a Convention right.[6] Furthermore, the HRA requires that primary and subordinate legislation must be read and given effect in a way that is compatible with the Convention rights.[7] Finally, individuals in the UK can bring a case to the European Court of Human Rights (ECtHR) alleging a breach of their Convention rights once they have exhausted all domestic remedies.

8. Historically, there was no constitutional basis for the right to privacy in the UK.[8] A recognition of such a right has also been slow. Indeed, the turning point for the recognition of the importance of the protection of personal privacy in the UK was the implementation of the Human Rights Act 1998.[9] Before this, the protection of what are considered privacy-related rights has evolved in the UK mainly through torts law.[10] More particularly, two actions have been relevant in this respect: 'breach of confidence' and – to an extent – 'defamation'. Early court cases demonstrated a reluctance from the judiciary to recognise an independent cause of action for the invasion of privacy.[11] For instance, in *Kaye v. Robertson*,[12] a case which concerned a tabloid journalist entering a hospital and obtaining photographs of an injured actor, Glidewell LJ noted that:

> It is well-known that in English law there is no right to privacy, and accordingly there is no right of action for breach of a person's privacy. The facts of the present case are a graphic illustration of the desirability of Parliament considering whether and in what circumstances statutory provision can be made to protect the privacy of individuals.

---

3. *See also* below.
4. O'Cinneide, *Human rights and the UK constitution, supra*, 7.
5. *Ibid.*
6. Section 6 of the HRA.
7. Section 3 of the HRA.
8. Orla Lynskey, Courts, privacy and data protection in the UK: Why two wrongs don't make a right 216 (Maja Brkan and Enangelia Psychogiopoulou eds. Courts, Privacy and Data Protection in the Digital Environment, Edward Elgar 2017).
9. Rosemary Jay, *Data Protection Law and Practice* 2 (Sweet & Maxwell 5th Ed. 2020).
10. *Wainwright v. Home Office* [2004] 2 AC 406.
11. Lynskey, *supra*.
12. [1990] EWCA Civ 21, [1991] FSR 62.

9. As mentioned above, the incorporation of the ECHR in the UK legal order through the adoption of the HRA 1998 marked a turning point for the gradual recognition of privacy rights in the UK. In *Campbell v. MGN Ltd*, a landmark case, the House of Lords established the tort action for 'misuse of private information'.[13] As Lord Nicholls noted:

> In this country, … there is no over-arching, all-embracing cause of action for 'invasion of privacy'. But protection of various aspects of privacy is a fast developing area of the law, here and in some other common law jurisdictions …[14] The present case concerns one aspect of invasion of privacy: wrongful disclosure of private information. The case involves the familiar competition between freedom of expression and respect for an individual's privacy. Both are vitally important rights. Neither has precedence over the other. The importance of freedom of expression has been stressed often and eloquently, the importance of privacy less so. But it, too, lies at the heart of liberty in a modern state. A proper degree of privacy is essential for the well-being and development of an individual. And restraints imposed on government to pry into the lives of the citizen go to the essence of a democratic state.[15]

10. Lord Nichols considered that 'information about an individual's private life would not, in ordinary usage, be called "confidential". The more natural description today is that such information is private' and, therefore, the continuing use of the phrase 'duty of confidence' is not appropriate. Thus, 'the essence of the tort is better encapsulated now as misuse of private information'.[16] In the *Campbell* judgment it was noted that the ECHR and the Strasbourg jurisprudence, 'have undoubtedly had a significant influence in this area of the common law for some years'.[17] Finally, *Campbell* is also seminal because it established[18] that Convention rights could apply indirectly to disputes between private individuals.[19]

---

13. [2004] UKHL 22.
14. *Ibid.*, 11.
15. *Ibid.*, 12.
16. *Ibid.*, 14.
17. *Ibid.*, 16.
18. *Ibid.*, 71.
19. Lynskey, *supra*, 224.

Chapter 2. National Application of Regional and International Conventions

11. As mentioned above, the roots of privacy protection in the UK were found in equity and tort law rather than in constitutional fundamental rights. Despite this lack of a constitutional basis, privacy and data protection have developed slowly over the years under the influence of the ECHR, the Council of Europe Convention for the Protection of Individuals with regard to Automatic Processing of Personal Data (Convention 108)[20] and the HRA 1998 which infused a rights-based approach in the jurisprudence of the British courts.[21]

12. Historically, the UK can be viewed as a relative 'late-starter'[22] regarding data protection as well. While various privacy bills were introduced into the UK Parliament during the 1960s and early 1970s[23] (data protection is a reserved matter, namely the same law applies across the devolved administrations), no data protection legislation was adopted until 1984. Despite the unsuccessful legislative attempts, there was a clear interest in data protection matters. In 1970, the then Labour Government appointed Kenneth Younger to Chair a Committee on Privacy. The 'Younger Report'[24] formulated the following ten principles on the handling of personal information in the context of computers use:

(a) The purpose of holding data should be specified.
(b) There should be authorised access only to data.
(c) There should be minimum holdings of data for specified purposes.
(d) Persons in statistical surveys should not be identified.
(e) Subject access to data should be given.
(f) There should be security precautions for data.
(g) There should be security procedures for personal data.
(h) Data should only be held for limited relevant periods.
(i) Data should be accurate and up to date.
(j) Any value judgments should be coded.

13. A few years later, in 1978, another Committee, the Lindop Committee, produced a Report[25] recommending data protection legislation covering both public and private sectors. The Lindop Report proposed that legislation reflects the interests of: (i) data subjects (e.g., data subjects should know what personal data relating to them are handled, why those data are needed, how they will be used, who will

20. ETS No. 108, 28/01/1981.
21. Lynskey, *supra*, 215.
22. Paul de Hert and Vagelis Papakonstantinou, *The rich UK contribution to the field of EU data protection: Let's not go for 'third country' status after Brexit*, 33 Computer Law & Security Review 354, 355 (2017).
23. Mr Lyon, 1967; Mr Walden, 1969; Kenneth Baker, 1968; Mr Huckfield, 1969; Lord Manocroft 1971.
24. Younger K, *Report of the Committee on privacy*, Cmnd. 5012, Her Majesty's Stationery Office, London 1972.
25. Lindop, *Report of the Committee on Data Protection*, cmnd. 7341, 1978.

use them, for what purpose, and for how long); (ii) 'users' ('users' should be able to handle personal data in the pursuit of their lawful interests or duties to the extent and for the purposes made known or authorised without undue extra cost in money or other resources); and (iii) the community at large (the community at large should enjoy any benefits, and be protected from any prejudice, which may flow from the handling of personal data). The Lindop Report also recommended the mandatory registration of computer users, the adoption of codes of conduct and the creation of an independent supervisory authority.

14. Eventually, the first piece of data protection legislation in the UK, the Data Protection Act 1984, was enacted in July 1984. The 1984 Act implemented Council of Europe (CoE) Convention 108[26] and drew on the Organisation for Economic Co-operation and Development (OECD) Guidelines on the Protection of Privacy and Transborder Flows of Personal Data 1980[27] and the work carried out by the Younger and the Lindop Committees.[28] The Data Protection Act 1984 laid down eight principles for data processing. It required that:

(1) personal data shall be obtained and processed fairly and lawfully;
(2) personal data shall be held only for specified and lawful purposes;
(3) personal data shall not be used or disclosed in a manner incompatible with these purposes;
(4) personal data shall be adequate, relevant and not excessive in relation to these purposes;
(5) personal data shall be accurate and where necessary kept up to date;
(6) personal data shall not be kept for longer than necessary for that purpose or these purposes;
(7) an individual shall be entitled to subject access;
(8) there shall be appropriate security measures for personal data.

15. It is worth noting that the 1984 Act did not make any mention of privacy or fundamental rights[29] – indeed, its long title was: 'An Act to regulate the use of automatically processed information relating to individuals and the provision of services in respect of such information.' Moreover, the 1984 Act was primarily driven by economic reasons.[30] As a commentator noted:

> In commending the first Data Protection Bill to the House of Commons the Home Secretary commented that it was designed "to meet public concern, to bring us into step with Europe and to protect our international, commercial and

---

26. ETS No. 108, 28/01/1981.
27. Guidelines on the Protection of Privacy and Transborder Flows of Personal Data (23 Sep. 1980) OECD Doc C(80)58/FINAL.
28. *See* Jay, *supra*, 13.
29. As Jay astutely observed, the 1984 Act 'turned its back on its roots' and 'pointedly ignored any questions of privacy'. *Ibid.*, 14.
30. Colin Bennett and Charles Raab, *The Governance of Privacy: Policy Instruments in Global Perspective*, 68 (MIT Press 2006).

trading interests". Whilst undoubtedly civil libertarian concerns are fundamental to the concept of data protection it is significant that these represented only one out of five interests identified and that, at least numerically, commercial and trading factors assumed greater significance.[31]

16. The successor of the 1984 Act, the 1998 Data Protection Act, which incorporated the EU Data Protection Directive[32] into the UK, followed a similar approach and did not mention privacy either.[33] Indeed, the long title of this document was: 'An Act to make new provision for the regulation of the processing of information relating to individuals, including the obtaining, holding, use or disclosure of such information.'

17. Even more recently, as Lord Justice Leveson observed, data protection in the UK is seen as:

> little known or understood by the public, regarded as a regulatory inconvenience in the business world, and viewed as marginal and technical among practitioners (including our higher courts).[34]

18. Similarly, other scholars have commented that: 'UK privacy leaders generally framed privacy protection as a form of risk management to avoid harm to consumer expectations' and 'often define privacy protection in terms of fairness to customers and employees and managing risk'.[35] This approach differs strikingly from continental European approaches that view privacy and data protection as constitutional fundamental rights.[36]

19. A closer look at the UK courts' jurisprudence on data protection reveals a similar mixed picture. In *Durant v. FSA*,[37] the Court of Appeal held that 'personal data' could be considered only information 'biographical in a significant sense' or which affected the privacy of an individual.[38] The Court of Appeal justified this restrictive interpretation of personal data[39] by noting that the Data Protection Act 1998 (DPA 1998) which implemented the Data Protection Directive in the UK was intended to give effect to the requirements of Article 8 ECHR. In more recent case law, however, the UK courts have indicated willingness to pay due account to EU

31. Ian Lloyd, *Information Technology Law*, 38 (Second edition, Oxford University Press 2004).
32. Directive 95/46/EC of the European Parliament and of the Council of 24 Oct. 1995 on the Protection of Individuals With Regard to the Processing of Personal Data and on the Free Movement of Such Data [1995] OJ L 281/31.
33. *See* Jay, *supra*, 14.
34. Lord Justice Leveson, *An Inquiry into the Culture, Practices and Ethics of the Press*, 999 (London 2012).
35. Kenneth Bamberger and Deirdre Mulligan, *Privacy on the Ground, Driving Corporate Behaviour in the United States and Europe*, 6 and 12 (MIT Press 2015).
36. *Ibid*. *See also* de Hert and Papakonstantinou, *supra*, 357.
37. [2003] EWCA Civ 1746.
38. *Ibid*., para. 16.
39. Its effects have now been limited. *See Edem v. IC & Financial Services Authority* [2014] EWCA Civ 92.

data protection law, including the EU Charter of Fundamental Rights. In *Google Inc v. Vidal Hall*,[40] the Court of Appeal had to consider the operation of what has become known as the 'Safari workaround'. In particular, the claimants were three individuals who used Apple computers between the summer of 2011 and February 2012. Each of them accessed the internet using their Apple Safari browser. The essence of their complaint was that Google collected private information about the claimants' internet usage via their Apple Safari browser (the Browser-Generated Information or BGI) without the claimants' knowledge and consent, by using a small string of text saved on the users' device ('cookies'). The cookies allowed Google to recognise the browser sending the BGI. The BGI was then aggregated and used by Google as part of its commercial offering to advertisers via its 'double-click' advertising service. This meant advertisers could select advertisements targeted or tailored to the claimants' interests, as deduced from the collected BGI, which could be and were displayed on the screens of the claimants' computer devices. This revealed private information about the claimants, which was or might have been seen by third parties. The tracking and collation of the claimants' BGI was contrary to Google's publicly stated position that such activity could not be conducted for Safari users unless they had expressly allowed it to happen.

20. The Court of Appeal made some interesting remarks regarding the interpretation and application of EU law – the Data Protection Directive – in *Vidal Hall*. It held that BGI constitutes personal data under section 1(1)(a) of the DPA[41] and noted that:

> since what the Directive purports to protect is privacy rather than economic rights, it would be strange if the Directive could not compensate those individuals whose data privacy had been invaded by a data controller so as to cause them emotional distress (but not pecuniary damage). It is the distressing invasion of privacy which must be taken to be the primary form of damage (commonly referred to in the European context as 'moral damage') and the data subject should have an effective remedy in respect of that damage.[42]

40. [2015] EWCA Civ 311.
41. *Ibid.*, para. 115.
42. *Ibid.*, para. 77.

Chapter 3. Privacy in Electronic Communications (Including Rules Regarding Use of Cookies, Etc.)

21. The growth and development of electronic communications networks, ready availability of broadband services and the range of digital communication devices pose considerable governance challenges for safeguarding users' privacy and ensuring the confidentiality of communications. Mobile devices used by individuals in their daily interactions enable service providers to track and monitor online activities. Cookies and similar technologies enable information to be stored in user devices and transmit a wide range of information to be collected, shared and used for purposes of predicting behaviour and commercial advertising. Electronic communications are susceptible to interception and respect for individuals fundamental right to the confidentiality of their communications, private life and correspondence are at risk.[43] Intimate details about an individual, behaviour and lifestyle choices can be revealed through electronic communications data.[44]

22. Directive 2002/58/EC was implemented in the UK by the Privacy and Electronic Communications (EC Directive) Regulations 2003 (PECR 2003).[45] The Privacy and Electronic Communications (EC Directive) (Amendment) Regulations 2011 regarding remedies for breach of security, consent, cookies and marketing came into effect on 25 May 2011.[46] The PECR 2003 complements the UK GDPR and Data Protection Act 2018 (DPA 2018) by defining the obligations owed by providers of public electronic communication networks and public electronic communication services to users.

23. Following the UK's departure from the EU, the PECR has been amended by the Data Protection, Privacy and Electronic Communications (Amendments etc.) (EU Exit) Regulations 2019 (DPPEC Regulations). As the PECR 2003 is an EU-derived domestic legislation under the European Union (Withdrawal) Act 2018

43. *See* European Data Protection Supervisor, 'Opinion 6/2017 EDPS Opinion on the Proposal for a Regulation on Privacy and Electronic Communications (ePrivacy Regulation)' (24 Apr. 2017), Joint hearing in Case C-623/17 (Privacy International) with Joined Cases C-511/18 and C- 512/18 (La Quadrature du Net and Others) and Case C-520/18 (Ordre des barreaux francophones et germanophone and Others).
44. CJEU, Joined Cases C-293/12 and C-594/12, *Digital Rights Ireland Ltd v. Minister for Communications, Marine and Natural Resources and Others and Kärntner Landesregierung and Others* [GC], 8 Apr. 2014.
45. Directive 2002/58/EC of the European Parliament and of the Council of 12 July 2002 concerning the processing of personal data and the protection of privacy in the electronic communications sector, OJ L 201, 31.7.2002, p. 37; amended by Directive 2009/136/EC. Also note that the obligations in respect of confidentiality of communications were initially implemented by the Regulation of Investigatory Powers Act 2000. Currently, reference to be made to the Investigatory Powers Act 2016 (SI 2018/356) and Investigatory Powers (Interception by Businesses etc for Monitoring and Record Keeping Purposes) Regulations 2018. Directive 2002/58 has since been amended by Directive 2009/136 on 25th November 2009.
46. SI 2011/1208.

(EUWA 2018), the interpretive rules noted previously will be applied. Additionally, the DPPEC Regulations amend Article 95 of the UK GDPR as follows:[47]

> This Regulation shall not impose additional obligations on natural or legal persons in relation to processing in connection with the provision of publicly available electronic communications services in public communication networks in the United Kingdom in relation to matters for which they are subject to specific obligations with the same objective set out in domestic law made before IP completion day implementing Directive 2002/58/EC of the European Parliament and of the Council of 12th July 2002 concerning the processing of personal data and the protection of privacy in the electronic communications sector.

24. It is clear that the European Charter of Fundamental Rights will cease to be relevant to the interpretation of the PECR 2003. The focus, instead, when interpreting the scope of the PECR would be directed towards the UK Human Rights Act 1998 (HRA 1998). The UK is a signatory to the ECHR, and respecting the private and family life, home and correspondence is now part of the HRA 1998.[48] These matters apart, there are no substantive implications to the application of the PECR following the UK's departure. The DPPEC Regulations have not amended the regulations on cookies, direct marketing via email, telephone or fax, nuisance calls, as well as rules on safeguarding users'/subscribers' privacy as regards traffic and location data, itemised billing, line identification, and directory listings. The Information Commissioner has issued a draft code on direct marketing (version 1.0) and made available resources to enhance organisation's compliance with PECR 2003 obligations.[49] The discussion below will identify some of the notable changes made by the DPPEC Regulations.

§1. Definitions

25. The principal definitions, such as public electronic communications network and public electronic communications services, remain as do many of the terms in Regulation 2 PECR 2003. However, the following should be noted as they are relevant to issues raised by the use of cookies and other tracking technologies.

---

47. Words in Art. 95 substituted (31.12.2020) by The Data Protection, Privacy and Electronic Communications (Amendments etc) (EU Exit) Regulations 2019 (S.I. 2019/419), reg. 1(2), Sch. 1 para. 74(2) and (3) (with reg. 5); 2020 c. 1, Sch. 5 para. 1(1).
48. *See* Law Society, response to the Ministry of Justice 'Human Rights Act reform: A Modern Bill of Rights' consultation (March 2022) Available at: https://www.lawsociety.org.uk/campaigns/consultation-responses/human-rights-act-reform-a-modern-bill-of-rights-consultation-law-society-response.
49. *See* https://ico.org.uk/for-organisations/guide-to-pecr/.

26. 'Consent' by a user or subscriber will now mirror that of the data subject's consent in the UK GDPR (as defined in section 3(10) of the DPA 2018).[50] 'Location data' extends to any data processed in an electronic communications network as well as data processed by an electronic communications service indicating the geographical position of the terminal equipment of a user of a public electronic communications service.[51] Finally, 'personal data breach' means a breach of security leading to the accidental or unlawful destruction, loss, alteration, unauthorised disclosure of, or access to, personal data transmitted, stored or otherwise processed in connection with the provision of a public electronic communications service.[52] This definition mirrors Directive 2009/136.[53] Recital 57 emphasises that:

> The provider of a publicly available electronic communications service should take appropriate technical and organisational measures to ensure the security of its services. Without prejudice to Directive 95/46/EC, such measures should ensure that personal data can be accessed only by authorised personnel for legally authorised purposes, and that the personal data stored or transmitted, as well as the network and services, are protected. Moreover, a security policy with respect to the processing of personal data should be established in order to identify vulnerabilities in the system, and monitoring and preventive, corrective and mitigating action should be regularly carried out.

27. Regulation 5 PECR 2003 imposes on providers of public electronic communications services some significant obligations, principally involving the maintenance of proper security for systems and security breach notifications.[54] The Information Commissioner has provided guidance in the document, Notification of PECR Security Breaches (version 2.2) which continues to be relevant when interpreting the enhanced security obligations under Regulation 5 PECR 2003.[55] The new Regulation 5(1A) provides that the measures to be adopted by providers of public electronic communications services include those relating to the scope and authority of personnel accessing personal data; safeguarding against accidental or unlawful destruction, accidental loss or alteration, and unauthorised or unlawful storage; processing, access or disclosure; and ensuring the implementation of a

---

50. Words in reg. 2(1) inserted (29.3.2019) by The Data Protection, Privacy and Electronic Communications (Amendments etc) (EU Exit) Regulations 2019 (S.I. 2019/419), regs 1(3), 8(2).
51. Words in reg. 2 inserted (26.5.2011) by The Privacy and Electronic Communications (EC Directive) (Amendment) Regulations 2011 (S.I. 2011/1208), regs 1(1), 3(a).
52. Words in reg. 2 inserted (26.5.2011) by The Privacy and Electronic Communications (EC Directive) (Amendment) Regulations 2011 (S.I. 2011/1208), regs 1(1), 3(b).
53. Directive 2009/136/EC of the European Parliament and of the Council of 25 Nov. 2009 amending Directive 2002/22/EC on universal service and users' rights relating to electronic communications networks and services, Directive 2002/58/EC concerning the processing of personal data and the protection of privacy in the electronic communications sector and Regulation (EC) No. 2006/2004 on cooperation between national authorities responsible for the enforcement of consumer protection laws (Text with EEA relevance).
54. *See* Directive 2009/136.
55. Available at https://ico.org.uk/for-organisations/guide-to-pecr/communications-networks-and-services/security-breaches/.

security policy with respect to the processing of personal data.[56] The Information Commissioner has provided a template which can be used by providers to set out an inventory of data security measures and breaches. Regulation 5(6) PECR 2003 gives the Information Commissioner the power to audit service provider's compliance with its security obligations.[57] Regulations 5A-C PECR 2003 set out framework for enhanced personal data breach obligations, which include notification, audit and enforcement.[58] The amount of a fixed monetary penalty for non-compliance shall be GBP 1,000.

28. There are no substantive changes to Regulation 6 other than the fact that the definition of consent corresponds to that of the data subject's consent in Article 4(1) of the UK GDPR which means:

> any freely given, specific, informed and unambiguous indication of the data subject's wishes by which he or she, by a statement or by a clear affirmative action, signifies agreement to the processing of personal data relating to him or her.

29. Directive 2009/136 makes reference to the use of browser settings as signifying consent is made explicit in Regulation 6(3A).[59] Consent to storing or gaining access to information stored in the terminal equipment of a subscriber or user will not be prohibited if undertaken for the sole purpose of carrying out the transmission of a communication over an electronic communications network; or where such storage or access is strictly necessary for the provision of an information society service requested by the subscriber or user.[60]

30. The European Commission published its proposal for an e-Privacy Regulation.[61] The proposal will repeal and replace Directive 2002/58/EC on privacy and electronic communications. The e-Privacy Regulation will extend the scope of Directive 2002/58/EC to regulate all electronic communications service providers, including WhatsApp, Facebook messenger, Skype, Gmail and iMessage. The e-Privacy Regulation will enhance the security and communications confidentiality obligations. The e-Privacy Regulation will also seek to clarify the application of electronic direct marketing rules and aim to promote greater harmonisation among

56. Reg. 5(1A) inserted (26.5.2011) by The Privacy and Electronic Communications (EC Directive) (Amendment) Regulations 2011 (S.I. 2011/1208), regs 1(1), 4(1).
57. Reg. 5(6) inserted (26.5.2011) by The Privacy and Electronic Communications (EC Directive) (Amendment) Regulations 2011 (S.I. 2011/1208), regs 1(1), 4(2).
58. Regulations 5A-5C inserted (26.5.2011) by The Privacy and Electronic Communications (EC Directive) (Amendment) Regulations 2011 (S.I. 2011/1208), regs 1(1), 5.
59. Also note the specific requirements under Art. 7 of the UK GDPR.
60. Regulation 6(2)(b) substituted (26.5.2011) by The Privacy and Electronic Communications (EC Directive) (Amendment) Regulations 2011 (S.I. 2011/1208), regs 1(1), 6(3).
61. Proposal for a Regulation of the European Parliament and of the Council concerning the respect for private life and the protection of personal data in electronic communications and repealing Directive 2002/58/EC (Regulation on privacy and electronic communications), COM(2017) 10 final, 2017/0003 (COD).

Member States in their implementation of rules on metadata, and tracking/ monitoring technologies. As the e-Privacy Regulation was not operational before the end of the transitional period, its rules will not be directly applicable in the UK. That said, the European Union (Withdrawal) Act 2018 does have some degree of flexibility to mirror the e-Privacy Regulation – a necessary feature if issues about adequacy are not raised by the European Commission. On a final note, when the e-Privacy Regulation becomes operational, it will have to be complied with by organisations processing electronic communications data that are either established/ located in EU or processing EU users'/subscribers' personal data.

Chapter 4. Other Relevant National Legal Provisions Regarding the Protection of Privacy (Not In-Depth Analysis but Overview; In-Depth Analysis in Part X)

31. There are two further legal regimes concerning the protection of personal data in UK law: one is applicable to the processing of personal data for law enforcement purposes[62] and the other to processing by 'intelligence services'.[63] The legal framework for the processing of personal data for law enforcement purposes is set out in Part 3 of the DPA 2018, which was enacted to implement the LED. The legal regime for the processing of personal data by 'intelligence services' is regulated by Part 4 of the DPA 2018. These frameworks are separate from the general data processing regime (UK GDPR).

62. *See* below Part X: Chapter 3.
63. *See* below Part X: Chapter 4.

Part II. National Data Protection Law

Chapter 1. Background: General Description of the National Data Protection Law

32. The United Kingdom withdrew from the European Union on 31 January 2020. On the basis of the Agreement on the withdrawal of the United Kingdom of Great Britain and Northern Ireland from the European Union and the European Atomic Energy Community, Union law continued to apply in the United Kingdom during the transition period until 31 December 2020.[64] Prior to the withdrawal and during the transition period, the regulatory framework on the protection of personal data in the United Kingdom comprised of relevant EU legislation (in particular Regulation (EU) 2016/679, Privacy and Electronic Communications Regulation (SI 2003/2426) (PECR) and Directive (EU) 2016/680 of the European Parliament and of the Council[65]) and national legislation, in particular, the DPA 2018 which provided national rules, where permitted by Regulation 2016/679, restricting its application and transposed Regulation 2016/680.

33. The UK Government enacted the European Union (Withdrawal) Act 2018, as part of its preparation for leaving the EU. The broad goal of the EUWA is that all direct Union legislation which was incorporated into UK law at the end of the transition period is incorporated into UK law as it has effect in EU law immediately before the end of the transition period.[66] One consequence of the extension of the transitional period for twelve months after Exit Day was that EU law continued to be applied in the UK, including cases decided by the Court of Justice of the European Union (CJEU). Not only were cases decided by the CJEU treated as retained EU law, but the interpretive rules under the EUWA 2018 will apply unless the UK has adopted an alternative set of provisions. From a data protection perspective

64. Agreement on the withdrawal of the United Kingdom of Great Britain and Northern Ireland from the European Union and the European Atomic Energy Community 2019/C 384 I/01, XT/21054/2019/INIT, (OJ C 384I, 12.11.2019, p. 1), available at the following link: https://eur-lex.europa.eu/legal- content/EN/TXT/PDF/?uri=CELEX:12019W/TXT(02)&from=EN.
65. Directive (EU) 2016/680 of the European Parliament and of the Council of 27 Apr. 2016 on the protection of natural persons with regard to the processing of personal data by competent authorities for the purposes of the prevention, investigation, detection or prosecution of criminal offences or the execution of criminal penalties, and on the free movement of such data, and repealing Council Framework Decision 2008/977/JHA (OJ L 119, 4.5.2016, pages 89), available at the following link: https://eur-lex.europa.eu/legal-content/EN/TXT/PDF/?uri=CELEX:32016L0680&from=EN.
66. *See* s. 3 of the European Union (Withdrawal) Act 2018.

there are now two strands to EU-derived legislation. The first covers domestic legislation that is 'EU derived' (e.g., applied GDPR, DPA 2018 Part 3), and the second being direct EU legislation, which includes the GDPR.[67]

34. It is worth highlighting the following extract from the Explanatory Notes to the European Union (Withdrawal) Act 2018 which states that:

> Where legislation is converted under this Section, it is the text of the legislation itself which will form part of domestic legislation. This will include the full text of any EU instrument (including its recitals).[68]

35. A point worth bearing in mind, and reinforced by the Information Commissioner, is that recitals do not have the status of binding legal rules but are regarded as being an aide to clarification. The recitals in the UK GDPR have, therefore, as a consequence, not been amended, as in the way a number of articles in Articles of Regulation 2016/679 have been amended by the DPPEC Regulations.

36. There are some notable consequences for the development of UK data protection law following Exit Day.

37. Under the EUWA the ministers of the United Kingdom will have the power to introduce secondary legislation, via statutory instruments, to make the necessary modifications to retained EU law. An example of the power being exercised to make amendments can be seen in the range of amendments facilitated by the Data Protection, Privacy and Electronic Communications (Amendments etc.) (EU Exit) Regulations 2019 (DPPEC Regulations).[69] The DPPEC Regulations permit amendments to Regulation 2016/679 to reflect the changed status in the relationship between the UK and the EU. The DPPEC Regulations were used to make further amendments, remove particular provisions in the UK GDPR, provide a framework for exemptions and insert provisions which recognise European Economic Area (EEA) Member states. A number of the amendments to the UK GDPR and DPA 2018 involve deleting references to 'Member States' or making adjustments to adjusting terminology, such as replacing references to Regulation (EU) 2016/679 by references to the UK GDPR.[70] The Charter of Fundamental Rights is not classified as retained EU law and therefore would not be relevant to the interpretation of other retained EU law or form part of UK law.[71] The supremacy of EU law doctrine will not apply to the interpretation of provisions in the DPA 2018.

---

67. Note also the retained EU law version of the e-Privacy Directive (2002/58/EC) and the retained EU law version of the Network and Information Security Directive ((EU 2016/1148).
68. Explanatory Notes to the European Union (Withdrawal) Act 2018, para. 83, available at: https://www.legislation.gov.uk/ukpga/2018/16/pdfs/ukpgaen_20180016_en.pdf.
69. The Data Protection, Privacy and Electronic Communications (Amendments etc.) (EU Exit) Regulations 2019, available at the following link: https://www.legislation.gov.uk/uksi/2019/419/contents/made, as amended by the DPPEC Regulations 2020, available at: https://www.legislation.gov.uk/ukdsi/2020/9780348213522.
70. As an example *see* s. 17A of the DPA 2018.
71. EUWA 2018 s. 5(4).

38. Finally, the Information Commissioner is provided with powers under sections 121 to 125 of the DPA 2018 to prepare codes of practice on data sharing, direct marketing, age-appropriate design and data protection and journalism. Although codes of practice are not of a legally binding nature, the guidance carries interpretative weight in judicial proceedings and can be enforced by the Commissioner in practice. The Information Commissioner's Office (ICO) has since issued guidance with regard to the data protection implications following the end of the transition period.[72]

39. The UK is now a third country, in the sense that the European Commission's confirmation that the UK's data protection standards are comparable to those of the EU. The adequacy of the UK's data protection rules will continue to be a live issue where there are transborder flows of personal data. Binding corporate rules (BCRs) and transborder data sharing operations will have to be commensurate with EU GDPR standards.[73] Under Article 45 of the GDPR the adoption of an adequacy decision involves a proposal from the European Commission, an opinion of the European Data Protection Board (EDPB), approval from representatives of EU countries, and the adoption of the decision by the European Commission. On 28 June 2021, the EU Commission announced the approval of the UK's adequacy.[74] As the former Information Commissioner, Elizabeth Denham, observed:

> Approved adequacy means that businesses can continue to receive data from the EU without having to make any changes to their data protection practices. Adequacy is the best outcome as it means organisations can carry on with data protection as usual. And people will continue to enjoy the protections that their data will be used fairly, lawfully and transparently.[75]

40. There are a number of additional points to be noted with regard to the adoption of the adequacy decision:

41. First, given that the UK's data protection system is based on the same rules that were applicable when the UK was a Member State of the EU, the principles, rights and obligations of the GDPR and the LED continue to be maintained.

---

72. *See* https://ico.org.uk/for-organisations/dp-at-the-end-of-the-transition-period/overview-data-protection-and-the-eu/.
73. *See* for background to significance of adequacy issues: Case C-311/18, *Maximilian Schrems v. Data Protection Commissioner* ('*Schrems II*') ECLI:EU:C:2020:559.
74. European Commission, COMMISSION IMPLEMENTING DECISION of 28.6.2021 pursuant to Regulation (EU) 2016/679 of the European Parliament and of the Council on the adequate protection of personal data by the United Kingdom C(2021) 4800 final and COMMISSION IMPLEMENTING DECISION of 28.6.2021 pursuant to Directive (EU) 2016/680 of the European Parliament and of the Council on the adequate protection of personal data by the United Kingdom C(2021) 4801 final. *See also* https://ec.europa.eu/commission/presscorner/detail/en/ip_21_3183 and Guidance from Department for Digital, Culture, Media and Sport: https://www.gov.uk/guidance/using-personal-data-in-your-business-or-other-organisation#history.
75. *See* https://ico.org.uk/about-the-ico/news-and-events/news-and-blogs/2021/06/ico-statement-in-response-to-the-eu-commission-s-announcement-on-the-approval-of-the-uk-s-adequacy/.

42. Second, the UK continues to provide strong safeguards when personal data is processed by public authorities in the UK particularly when national security reasons are relied upon.[76] There is an expectation that appropriate mechanisms are put in place to ensure that surveillance and processing activities are necessary, proportionate and subject to judicial oversight.[77] One consequence of this expectation is that the UK will continue to be subject to the jurisdiction of the ECtHR and must adhere to the European Convention of Human Rights as well as to the Council of Europe Convention for the Protection of Individuals with regard to Automatic Processing of Personal Data.

43. Third, the adequacy decisions incorporate a 'sunset clause', which means that after four years, the findings will have to be renewed. This will mean that the adequacy findings can be suspended at any time should the Commission find that the UK has deviated from the level of protection currently in place.

44. Fourth, with regard to transfers of personal data for the purposes of UK immigration control,[78] these are excluded from the scope of the adequacy decision adopted under the GDPR. That said, the Commission is vested with the authority to assess the need for its continued exclusion.[79]

---

76. *See*, for example, UK Government Guidance on National Security Certificates, available at the following link: https://assets.publishing.service.gov.uk/government/uploads/system/uploads/attachment_data/file/9102 79/Data_Protection_Act_2018_-_National_Security_Certificates_Guidance.pdf.
77. *See* s. 35 of the DPA 2018, Part 3 of the Data Protection Act 2018 (DPA 2018) and Art. 35 of the Directive (EU) 2016/680. On redress *see* s. 165 of the DPA 2018. Also note the role of common law powers: *R(Catt) v. Association of Chief Police Officers* [2015] AC 1065.
78. *See* para. 4(1) of Sch. 2 to the UK DPA 2018.
79. The implications of this ruling render the position at present less than clear: *Court of Appeal (Civil Division), Open Rights Group v. Secretary of State for the Home Department and Secretary of State for Digital, Culture, Media and Sport*, [2021] EWCA Civ 800, paragraphs 53 to 56. The High Court of Justice's decision assessed the exemption in light of Regulation (EU) 2016/679 (in particular, its Art. 23) and the Charter of Fundamental Rights of the European Union and found the exemption to be lawful (*Open Rights Group & Anor, R (On the Application Of) v. Secretary of State for the Home Department & Anor* [2019] EWHC 2562). This decision was reversed in the Court of Appeal.

Chapter 2. Scope of the National Law (Material, Personal, Territorial)

45. Like Regulation 2016/679, the UK GDPR applies to the processing of personal data of living individuals wholly or partly by automated means, or to other processing, if the personal data forms part of a filing system.[80] The material, personal and territorial scope following Brexit is determined by reference to the UK GDPR and DPA 2018 as amended by the DPPEC Regulations. Key definitions in the UK GDPR have not been amended by the DPPEC Regulations and concepts such as 'personal data', 'data subject' and 'processing' continue to mirror those contained in Regulation 2016/679.[81] The data protection regime covers the processing of information relating to living individuals. Similarly to what is provided under Regulation (EU) 2016/679, the UK GDPR does not apply to the processing of personal data by an individual in the course of a purely personal or household activity.[82] The scope of purely personal or household activity would presumably include those which were enacted by the DPA 1998, when implementing Directive 95/46/EC:

> Personal data processed by an individual only for the purposes of that individual's personal, family or household affairs (including recreational purposes) are exempt from the data protection principles and the provisions of Parts II and III.[83]

46. It is worth noting that the EU GDPR will continue to be relevant where there are transborder flows of personal data and processing operations of controllers and processors who have establishments in EU Member States. We can infer this to be the case as the EU GDPR covers controllers and processors whether the processing takes place in the Union or not in the context of the activities of an establishment of a controller or a processor in the Union.[84]

47. Article 3(1) of the UK GDPR states that the data protection rules apply to the processing of personal data in the context of the activities of an establishment of a controller or a processor in the United Kingdom.

48. A number of further points need to be noted. The DPPEC Regulations make a number of amendments to Article 2 to reflect the data protection regime in the UK post-Brexit. The rules and principles governing the processing of personal data by a competent authority for any of the law enforcement purposes are set out in the DPA 2018. The processing of manual unstructured personal data is now covered by

80. Article 2(1) and (5) of the UK GDPR.
81. Article 4(1) and (2) of the UK GDPR.
82. Article 2(2)(a) of the UK GDPR.
83. CJEU, C-101/01, Criminal proceedings against Bodil Lindqvist, 6 Nov. 2003, CJEU, C-212/13, *František Ryneš v. Úřad pro ochranu osobních údajů*, 11 Dec. 2014, *Tietosuojavaltuutettu v. Jehovan todistajat – uskonnollinen yhdyskunta* (Case C-25/17) EU:C:2018:57, 10 July 2018 and *Sergejs Buivids* (Case C-345/17).
84. Article 3(1) of the EU GDPR.

the UK GDPR. Article 2(1A) of the UK GDPR states that such forms of personal data held by a freedom of information (FOI) public authority[85] will be brought within the data protection regime. Processing by Law Enforcement and Intelligence Services continues to be regulated by the DPA 2018 (Part 3 and Part 4). The UK GDPR and DPA 2018 apply throughout the UK as data protection is not a devolved matter. Both these instances of processing fall outside the scope of the GDPR.

49. The UK GDPR also extends its scope to processing in the course of an activity which, immediately before the end of the transition period, fell outside the scope of European Union law (e.g., national security) or was within the scope of Chapter 2 of Title 5 of the Treaty on European Union (Common Foreign and Security Policy activities). The data processing operations are set out in Article 2(1)(a) and (b) of the UK GDPR.

50. The UK GDPR will apply to national security activities to the extent that they are not undertaken by a competent authority for law enforcement purposes. In most instances, Part 3 of the DPA 2018 will apply or where the activities are specifically removed from the material reach of the UK GDPR and will be subject to Part 4 of the DPA 2018 pursuant to Article 2(2)(c) of the UK GDPR.[86] A typical scenario would be security checks made by the police force in respect of an employee seeking access to national security material. The processing in question is arguably not one which can be regarded as coming within the category of a law enforcement purpose, albeit the fact that the police force is a competent authority. In such an instance, the UK GDPR and not the DPA 2018 will apply. It remains to be seen how concerns about the legitimacy, necessity and proportionality of processing of personal data by a competent authority for purposes of prevention, investigation and detection of criminal offences will be addressed in the post-Brexit UK.[87] The UK GDPR does not apply to the processing of personal data by a competent authority for law enforcement purposes, including safeguarding against and the prevention of threats to public security. Processing of personal data will be covered by Part 3 of the DPA 2018, as is the case for Directive (EU) 2016/680 under European Union law. Processing of personal data by intelligence services such as the Secret Intelligence Service and the Government Communications Headquarters will be covered by Part 4 of the DPA 2018.[88]

---

85. The definition of an 'FOI public authority' is provided in s. 21(5) of the DPA 2018, which includes any public authority as defined by the Freedom of Information Act 2000, or any Scottish public authority as defined in the Freedom of Information (Scotland) Act 2002 (asp 13).
86. *See* UK Explanatory Framework for Adequacy Discussions, section H: National Security Data Protection and Investigatory Powers Framework, page 8, available at the following link https://assets.publishing.service.gov.uk/government/uploads/system/uploads/attachment_data/file/872239/H_-_National_Security.pdf.
87. *See* CJEU, Joined Cases C-293/12 and C-594/12, *Digital Rights Ireland Ltd v. Minister for Communications, Marine and Natural Resources and Others and Kärntner Landesregierung and Others [GC]*, 8 Apr. 2014 and CJEU, Joined Cases C-203/15 and C-698/15, *Tele2 Sverige AB v. Post- och telestyrelsen and Secretary of State for the Home Department v. Tom Watson and Others [GC]*, 21 Dec. 2016.
88. Article 2(2)(b) and (c) of the UK GDPR.

51. Article 3 of the UK GDPR now sets out the territorial scope of processing for the purposes of UK law. These cover processing:

> By a controller or processor in the context of the activities of an establishment of a controller or a processor in the United Kingdom, regardless of whether the processing takes place in the United Kingdom or not.
>
> By a controller or processor not established in the United Kingdom in respect of processing activities related to the offering of goods or services, irrespective of whether a payment of the data subject is required, to such data subjects in the United Kingdom; or the monitoring of their behaviour as far as their behaviour takes place within the United Kingdom.
>
> By a controller not established in the United Kingdom, but in a place where domestic law applies by virtue of public international law.[89]

52. The UK GDPR extends to the processing of personal data (regardless of where it takes place) in the context of the activities of an establishment of a controller or a processor in the United Kingdom as well as to the processing of personal data of data subjects who are in the United Kingdom, where the processing activities are related to the offering of goods or services to such data subjects or the monitoring of their behaviour. Article 3(3) of the UK GDPR states that the processing of personal data by a controller and not established in the United Kingdom, but in a place where domestic law applies by virtue of public international law is covered by the regulation.[90]

53. The concept of 'establishment' has been the subject of judicial reasoning cases such as *Costeja v. Google*, *Weltimmo* and *Wirtschaftsakadamie v. Schleswig-Holstein*.[91] The definition of the concept in Recital 22 GDPR seeks to advocate a purposive approach and may inform the meaning to be attributed to the term 'establishment'. It is not entirely clear whether the creation of a domain name for a website would by itself be sufficient.[92] Neither is it entirely clear what will constitute processing of personal data in the context of an establishment.[93] For present purposes, section 207(7) of the DPA 2018 provides a non-exhaustive list identifying those who will be regarded as a controller or processor established in the UK:

- an individual who is regarded being ordinarily resident in the United Kingdom;
- a legal entity incorporated under the law of the United Kingdom or a part of the United Kingdom;

---

89. *See also* s. 207(2) and (3) of the DPA 2018.
90. *See*, for example, the Diplomatic Privileges Act 1964 and the 1961 Vienna Convention on Diplomatic Relations. Also *Basfar* (Respondent) *v. Wong* (Appellant) [2020] UKEAT/0223/19 on scope of diplomatic immunity. The CPS has provided guidance on diplomatic Immunity and diplomatic premises: https://www.cps.gov.uk/legal-guidance/diplomatic-immunity-and-diplomatic-premises.
91. C-131/12, C-230/14 and C-191/15.
92. *See VFK v. Amazon* EU C-191/15.
93. Given the rationale for protecting the rights of data subjects with regard to the processing of personal data, the ruling in *Google LLC v. CNIL* C-507/17 may be useful.

- a partnership or other unincorporated association formed under the law of the United Kingdom or a part of the United Kingdom; and
- a person (legal or natural) not within the above categories but who maintains and carries on activities through an office, branch or agency or other stable arrangements in the United Kingdom.

54. In passing, it should be noted that this approach is already evidenced in Article 3 of the EU GDPR.

55. Where controllers or processors are not established in the UK, a representative must be designated in writing.[94] Article 27(2) of the UK GDPR exempts from this obligation processing which is occasional, does not include, on a large scale, processing of special categories of data as referred to in Article 9(1) or processing of personal data relating to criminal convictions and offences referred to in Article 10. The onus is on the controller or processor to demonstrate that the absence in designating a representative is unlikely to result in a risk to the rights and freedoms of natural persons, taking into account the nature, context, scope and purposes of the processing; or that it is a public authority or body. A 'representative' can be a natural or legal person established in the Union. The role of the representative under Article 27 is to represent the controller or processor with regard to their respective obligations under the EU GDPR.[95]

56. Under Article 27(4) of the UK GDPR, the designated representative:

> shall be mandated by the controller or processor to be addressed in addition to or instead of the controller or the processor by, in particular, the Commissioner and data subjects, on all issues related to processing, for the purposes of ensuring compliance with [EU GDPR].
>
> The appointment of a representative under Article 27 of the UK GDPR 'shall be without prejudice to legal actions which could be initiated against the controller or the processor themselves'.

94. *See* rules on appointing a representative in Art. 27(1), (2), (4) and (5) of the UK GDPR.
95. Article 4(17) of the UK GDPR.

Chapter 3. Concepts and Definitions

57. This chapter sets out the most significant concepts and definitions employed in the UK data protection regime. Before turning to these, a brief reference should be made with regard to the interplay between the DPA 2018 and the UK GDPR. The DPA 2018 provides a large number of definitions, some of which can be regarded as broadly equivalent to those set out in the UK GDPR, while others provide an amended definition. For example, the concept of personal data, which is defined in Article 4(1), is worded differently in section 3(2) and (3) of the DPA 2018. Section 3(2) of the DPA states that personal data means 'any information relating to an identified or identifiable living individual'. However, the definition needs to be read alongside section 3(14)(c). Section 3(3) of the DPA 2018 states a 'living individual' for the purposes of defining the scope of personal data is someone 'who can be identified, directly or indirectly, in particular by reference to an identifier such as a name, an identification number, location data or an online identifier, or one or more factors specific to the physical, physiological, genetic, mental, economic, cultural or social identity of the individual'. Similarly, 'processing' section 3(4) of the DPA 2018 adopts a different wording ('information' rather than 'personal data') to Article 4(2) of the UK GDPR but in substance covers the scope.[96]

58. Section 4 Part 2 provides additional guidance with regard to the processing of personal data. Chapter 1 is relevant to most of the processing of personal data. Chapter 2 Part 2, for example, reiterates the fact that UK GDPR rules apply to general processing of personal data. This chapter supplements and is to be read with the UK GDPR. Part 2 Chapter 3 provides another set of definitions with regard to certain categories of processing of personal data to which the GDPR does not apply (*see* section 21 of the DPA 2018) and makes provision for a regime broadly equivalent to the UK GDPR. It is worth observing Part 2 Chapter 2 contains an additional set of definitions which aim to clarify the meaning of certain terms in the UK GDPR. Section 6 defines the scope of the meaning of a 'controller'. Section 7 sets out the meaning of public authorities and public bodies for the purposes of processing operations. Section 9 makes clear that in respect of Article 8(1) of the UK GDPR (conditions applicable to child's consent in relation to information society services), references to '16 years' will now be read as references to '13 years', and the reference to 'information society services' will not include preventive or counselling services. Section 14 makes provision for the purposes of Article 22(2)(b) of the UK GDPR for significant decisions based solely on automated processing that is authorised by law and subject to safeguards for the data subject's rights, freedoms and legitimate interests.

59. The definition provision in Article 4(1) of the UK GDPR aims to make clear that 'the 2018 Act' means the DPA 2018 (A1), 'domestic law' means the law of the United Kingdom or of a part of the United Kingdom (A2), 'the Commissioner'

---

96. Other terms adopting a slightly different wording: 'consent', 'controller', 'processor'. 'Data subject' is defined in s. 3(5) of the DPA 2018 but integrated into definition of personal data under Art. 4(1) of the UK GDPR.

means the Information Commissioner (A3). Schedule 12 DPA 2018 makes provision for the Information Commissioner.[97]

60. Some brief observations can be made to the concepts and definitions, over and above the comments above, with regard to the interplay between the DPA 2018 and UK GDPR. Article 4 UK of the GDPR seems to make no material changes to definitions of 'personal data', 'processing', 'restriction of processing', 'profiling', 'pseudonymisation' or 'filing system'. Judicial pronouncements and guidance provided by the Information Commissioner and the EDPB will continue to be relevant, noting the status of EU rulings and advisory Opinions. The definition of controller, which is central to data protection regulations, does not mention the 'data controller', which has been a commonly used term. Article 4(7) of the UK GDPR defines a 'controller' as meaning a natural or legal person, public authority, agency or other body which, alone or jointly with others, determines the purposes and means of the processing of personal data. Section 6 of the 2018 Act focuses on the features relevant to attributing and allocating responsibility which is consistent with Article 4(7) and the contemporary understanding of the usage of the term.[98] There are technical amendments to the definitions under the UK GDPR to reflect the fact that the UK is a third country and not a Member State. Under Article 4(9) public authorities which may receive personal data in the framework of a particular inquiry in accordance with domestic law shall not be regarded as recipients.[99] A 'representative' is a natural or legal person who must be established in the United Kingdom.[100] Similarly, 'binding corporate rules' means personal data protection policies which adhered to by a controller or processor established in the United Kingdom for transfers or a set of transfers of personal data to a controller or processor in one or more third countries within a group of undertakings, or group of enterprises engaged in a joint economic activity.[101] The Information Commissioner continues to provide guidance and updates on BCRs approved.[102] Article 4 also inserts new definitions. For example, Article 4(28) states that references to a fundamental right or fundamental freedom (however expressed) are to a fundamental right or fundamental

---

97. Section 114 of the DPA 2018.
98. *See*, for example, ss 58 and 104 of the DPA 2018. Also the Crown and Parliament as controllers is covered in ss 209 and 210 of the DPA.
99. Words in Art. 4(9) substituted (31.12.2020) by The Data Protection, Privacy and Electronic Communications (Amendments etc) (EU Exit) Regulations 2019 (S.I. 2019/419), reg. 1(2), Sch. 1 para. 6(4) (with reg. 5); 2020 c. 1, Sch. 5 para. 1(1).
100. Words in Art. 4(17) substituted (31.12.2020) by The Data Protection, Privacy and Electronic Communications (Amendments etc) (EU Exit) Regulations 2019 (S.I. 2019/419), reg. 1(2), Sch. 1 para. 6(7) (with reg. 5); 2020 c. 1, Sch. 5 para. 1(1).
101. Words in Art. 4(20) substituted (31.12.2020) by The Data Protection, Privacy and Electronic Communications (Amendments etc) (EU Exit) Regulations 2019 (S.I. 2019/419), reg. 1(2), Sch. 1 para. 6(8) (with reg. 5); 2020 c. 1, Sch. 5 para. 1(1).
102. *See* guidance and information provided by Information Commissioner: https://ico.org.uk/for-organisations/binding-corporate-rules/.

freedom which continues to form part of domestic law on and after Internet Protocol (IP) completion day by virtue of section 4 of the European Union (Withdrawal) Act 2018, as the right or freedom is amended or otherwise modified by domestic law from time to time on or after IP completion day.[103]

103. Article 4(27)(28) inserted (31.12.2020) by The Data Protection, Privacy and Electronic Communications (Amendments etc) (EU Exit) Regulations 2019 (S.I. 2019/419), reg. 1(2), Sch. 1 para. 6(13) (with reg. 5) (as amended by S.I. 2020/1586, regs 1(2), 4(3)(b)); 2020 c. 1, Sch. 5 para. 1(1).

Part III. General Principles

Chapter 1. Data Quality Principles (Purpose Limitation, Proportionality, Etc.)

61. The principles relating to the processing of personal data in the UK GDPR are the same as the ones enshrined in Article 5 of the EU GDPR. Indeed, Article 5 of the UK GDPR is identical and does not introduce any amendments to Article 5 of the GDPR.[104] The following data protection principles are included in the UK GDPR:

(a) Lawfulness, fairness and transparency principle: personal data shall be processed lawfully, fairly and in a transparent manner in relation to the data subject (Article 5(1)(a) of the UK GDPR).[105]
(b) Purpose limitation principle: personal data shall be collected for specified, explicit and legitimate purposes and not further processed in a manner that is incompatible with those purposes (Article 5(1)(b) of the UK GDPR). The conditions on further compatible processing pursuant to Article 6(4) of GDPR have also been retained with no significant modifications.[106]
(c) Data minimisation principle: personal data shall be adequate, relevant and limited to what is necessary in relation to the purposes for which they are processed (Article 5(1)(c) of the UK GDPR).
(d) Accuracy principle: personal data shall be accurate and, where necessary, kept up to date (Article 5(1)(d) of the UK GDPR).
(e) Storage limitation principle: personal data shall be kept in a form which permits identification of data subjects for no longer than is necessary for the purposes for which the personal data are processed (Article 5(1)(e) of the UK GDPR).
(f) Integrity and confidentiality principle: personal data shall be processed in a manner that ensures appropriate security of the personal data, including protection against unauthorised or unlawful processing and against accidental loss, destruction or damage, using appropriate technical or organisational measures (Article 5(1)(f) of the UK GDPR).[107]

62. The above data protection principles were contained in the applied GDPR for the transitional period during which this was in effect and are currently included

104. Jay, *supra*, 355.
105. *See also* Arts. 13 and 14 of the UK GDPR which reproduce Arts. 13 and 14 of the GDPR.
106. *See* Art. 6(4) of UK GDPR.
107. *See also* Arts 32–34 of the UK GDPR which replicate without changes Arts 32–34 of the GDPR.

in the UK GDPR. The overarching accountability principle[108] is also included in the UK GDPR. Even post-Brexit, the EU GDPR still remains relevant for the interpretation and application of the data processing principles.[109] As mentioned by a commentator, practitioners in the UK now have to look at the relevant articles and possibly the recitals of the EU GDPR which relate to them as well as relevant case law, in order to interpret the data protection principles in the EU GDPR.[110] Equivalent but not identical provisions regarding the data processing principles are also applicable in the context of law enforcement and intelligence services processing under the DPA 2018.[111] In those contexts, certain limitations to the principles are applicable.[112]

63. The enforcement of the data protection principles is monitored by the ICO, which can use its enforcement powers, including the powers to issue enforcement notices and impose monetary penalties.[113] Individuals may also enforce their rights when affected by breach of these principles.[114] The ICO has issued a 'Guide on the GDPR' that addresses the data protection principles.[115] The UK courts have also adjudicated in several cases on a number of data protection principles,[116] mainly under the previous legal framework of the 1998 DPA and the Data Protection Directive.[117]

64. The DPA 2018 provides an exemption to the data protection principles where required for the purpose of safeguarding national security or for defence purposes.[118] This exemption applies to the data protection principles (except the principle of lawfulness). The exemption must be considered and invoked by the

108. Article 5(2) GDPR.
109. For a detailed commentary on Art. 5 of the EU GDPR *see* Cécile De Terwangne 'Article 5. Principles relating to processing of personal data' 309, Kuner et al. (eds.) *The EU General Data Protection Regulation (GDPR)- A Commentary* (OUP 2020).
110. Jay, *supra*, 355.
111. *See* Pts 3 and 4 of DPA 2018.
112. *See also* below. It should be noted that the provisions of Art. 5 GDPR and Art. 4 of the Law Enforcement Directive (LED) are not identical. Directive 2016/680/EU of the European Parliament and of the Council of 27 Apr. 2016 on the Protection of Natural Persons with Regard to the Processing of Personal Data by Competent Authorities for the Purposes of the Prevention, Investigation, Detection or Prosecution of Criminal Offences or the Execution of Criminal Penalties, and on the Free Movement of Such Data, and Repealing Council Framework Decision 2008/977/JHA, OJ L 119/89.
113. *See* below.
114. *See* below.
115. Information Commissioner's Office, 'Guide to the General Data Protection Regulation (GDPR)' 14–47, 2018.
116. *See* Jay, *supra*, Ch. 6.
117. Directive 95/46/EC of the European Parliament and of the Council of 24 Oct. 1995 on the Protection of Individuals With Regard to the Processing of Personal Data and on the Free Movement of Such Data [1995] OJ L 281/31.
118. Section 26 of the DPA 2018.

controller on a case-by-case basis. It must comply with human rights standards (the Human Rights Act 1998), according to which any interference with privacy rights should be necessary and proportionate in a democratic society.[119]

119. *See* ICO's guidance on the national security and defence exception, available at the following link https://ico.org.uk/for-organisations/guide-to-data-protection/guide-to-the-general-data-protection-regulation-gdpr/national-security-and-defence/.

Chapter 2. Legal Grounds for Processing Personal Data

65. The legal grounds for processing personal data are found in the law of the United Kingdom in the UK GDPR, and, for law enforcement and intelligence authorities' processing in Part 3 and Part 4 of the DPA 2018, respectively.[120]

66. Article 6(1) of the UK GDPR contains an identical provision to the one of Article 6(1) of the EU GDPR with regard to grounds of processing. More particularly, there are six grounds for lawful processing of personal data under the UK GDPR:

(a) the data subject has given consent to the processing of his or her personal data for one or more specific purposes;
(b) processing is necessary for the performance of a contract to which the data subject is party or in order to take steps at the request of the data subject prior to entering into a contract;
(c) processing is necessary for compliance with a legal obligation to which the controller is subject;
(d) processing is necessary in order to protect the vital interests of the data subject or of another natural person;
(e) processing is necessary for the performance of a task carried out in the public interest or in the exercise of official authority vested in the controller;
(f) processing is necessary for the purposes of the legitimate interests pursued by the controller or by a third party, except where such interests are overridden by the interests or fundamental rights and freedoms of the data subject which require protection of personal data, in particular where the data subject is a child.

67. Consent as a ground for lawful processing in the UK GDPR[121] must satisfy the same conditions as the ones provided for in Article 7 of the EU GDPR: where processing is based on consent, the controller must be able to demonstrate that the data subject has consented;[122] a written request for consent must be presented using clear and plain language;[123] the data subject should have the right to withdraw consent at any time;[124] and when assessing whether consent is freely given, it should be taken into account whether the performance of a contract is conditional on consent to the processing of personal data that is not necessary for the performance of

120. *See* below.
121. According to Art. 4(11) of the UK GDPR, Consent means any freely given, specific, informed and unambiguous indication of the data subject's wishes by which he or she, by a statement or by a clear affirmative action, signifies agreement to the processing of personal data relating to him or her.
122. Article 7(1) GDPR.
123. Article 7(2) GDPR.
124. Article 7(3) GDPR.

that contract.[125] Regarding the conditions applicable to a child's consent in relation to information society services, a child's consent is lawful when the child is at least 13 years old.[126]

68. Section 7 of the DPA 2018 lays down the meanings of 'public authority' and 'public body' for the purposes of the GDPR under the law of the United Kingdom.[127] Section 8 of the DPA 2018 complements Article 6(1)(e) GDPR by explaining the public interest ground. Pursuant to section 8 of the DPA 2018, the processing of personal data under Article 6(1)(e) of the UK GDPR (necessary for the performance of a task carried out in the public interest or in the exercise of the controller's official authority), includes processing of personal data that is necessary for the administration of justice, the exercise of a function of either House of Parliament, the exercise of a function conferred on a person by an enactment or rule of law, the exercise of a function of the Crown, a Minister of the Crown or a government department, or an activity that supports or promotes democratic engagement.

69. There are significant consequences in case of personal data processing without an appropriate legal ground. In such cases, the Information Commissioner can impose a fine under section 155 of the DPA 2018 and/or serve an enforcement notice to the controller requiring the establishment of an appropriate legal basis or the ceasing of processing.

---

125. Article 7(4) GDPR.
126. Section 9 of the DPA 2018. *See also* Art. 8 GDPR, which mentions '16 years old', but allowed Member States to provide by law 'for a lower age for those purposes provided that such lower age is not below 13 years'.
127. '(a) a public authority as defined by the Freedom of Information Act 2000, (b) a Scottish public authority as defined by the Freedom of Information (Scotland) Act 2002 (asp 13), and (c) an authority or body specified or described by the Secretary of State in regulations, subject to subsections (2), (3) and (4).

    (2) An authority or body that falls within subsection (1) is only a 'public authority' or 'public body' for the purposes of the GDPR when performing a task carried out in the public interest or in the exercise of official authority vested in it.'

Chapter 3. Special Categories of Personal Data

70. Special categories of personal data are, by nature, particularly sensitive in relation to fundamental rights and freedoms and, therefore, merit specific protection as the context of their processing could create significant risks to individuals' fundamental rights and freedoms.[128] In the UK legal framework, the specific rules applying to the processing of special categories of personal data are found in both the UK GDPR and the DPA 2018. Data controllers, therefore, should ensure that they comply with the requirements of both instruments when processing special categories of data.[129] The special categories of personal data are listed in Article 9(1) of the UK GDPR: personal data revealing racial or ethnic origin, political opinions, religious or philosophical beliefs, or trade union membership, and the processing of genetic data,[130] biometric data[131] for the purpose of uniquely identifying a natural person, data concerning health[132] or data concerning a natural person's sex life or sexual orientation.[133]

71. According to Article 9(1) of the UK GDPR, which follows Article 9(1) GDPR, the processing of special categories of data is in principle prohibited, unless a specific ground of processing under Article 9(2) of the UK GDPR applies. The GDPR's provisions under Article 9(2)(a), (c), (d), (e) and (f) are retained unchanged in the UK GDPR. Special categories of personal data can be processed: if the data subject has given explicit consent to the processing of those personal data for one or more specified purposes;[134] where processing is necessary to protect the vital interests of the data subject or of another natural person where the data subject is physically or legally incapable of giving consent;[135] where processing is carried out in the course of its legitimate activities with appropriate safeguards by a foundation, association or any other not-for-profit body with a political, philosophical, religious or trade union aim and on condition that the processing relates solely to the members or to former members of the body or to persons who have regular contact with it in connection with its purposes and that the personal data are not disclosed outside that body without the consent of the data subjects;[136] if processing relates to

---

128. *See* Recital 51 GDPR.
129. Jay, *supra*, 296.
130. According to s.205(1) of DPA 2018, 'genetic data' is defined as 'personal data relating to the inherited or acquired genetic characteristics of an individual which gives unique information about the physiology or the health of that individual and which results, in particular, from an analysis of a biological sample from the individual in question'. This definition does not differ substantially from the GDPR's definition in Art. 4(13) GDPR.
131. According to s.205(1) of DPA 2018, 'biometric data' means 'personal data resulting from specific technical processing relating to the physical, physiological or behavioural characteristics of an individual, which allows or confirms the unique identification of that individual, such as facial images or dactyloscopic data'. This definition does not differ substantially from the GDPR's definition in Art. 4(14) GDPR.
132. The definition provided in s. 205(1) of DPA 2018 is the same as the one in Art. 4(15) GDPR.
133. The same special categories of personal data are listed in Art. 9(1) GDPR.
134. Article 9(2)(a) GDPR.
135. Article 9(2)(c) GDPR.
136. Article 9(2)(d) GDPR.

personal data which are manifestly made public by the data subject;[137] and, where processing is necessary for the establishment, exercise or defence of legal claims or whenever courts are acting in their judicial capacity.[138]

72. The grounds for processing special categories of personal data laid down in Article 9(2)(b), (g), (h), (i) and (j) GDPR require authorisation under national law, and they have been specified in the DPA 2018.[139] More particularly, special categories of personal data can be processed in the field of employment, social security and social protection[140] if:

(a) the processing is necessary for the purposes of performing or exercising obligations or rights which are imposed or conferred by law on the controller or the data subject in connection with employment, social security or social protection; and
(b) when the processing is carried out, the controller has an 'appropriate policy document' in place.[141]

73. Furthermore, special categories of data may be processed if the processing is necessary for health or social care purposes,[142] namely preventive or occupational medicine, the assessment of the working capacity of an employee, medical diagnosis, the provision of health care or treatment, the provision of social care, or the management of health care systems or services or social care systems or services.[143] Processing for health or social care purposes under Article 9(2)(h) of the UK GDPR is subject to the conditions and safeguards referred to in Article 9(3) of the GDPR, including an obligation of secrecy. This includes circumstances in which processing is carried out by or under the responsibility of a health professional or a social work professional or by another person who, in the circumstances, owes a duty of confidentiality under an enactment or rule of law.[144]

74. In the case of processing special categories of data for protecting public health, including protecting against serious cross-border threats to health or ensuring high standards of quality and safety of health care and of medicinal products or medical devices,[145] the DPA 2018 lays down a requirement of necessity and provides that such processing should be carried out 'by or under the responsibility of a health professional'[146] or 'by another person who in the circumstances owes a duty of confidentiality under an enactment or rule of law'.[147] According to Article

137. Article 9(2)(e) GDPR.
138. Article 9(2)(f) GDPR.
139. *See* s. 10 and Part 1 of Sch. 1 DPA 2018.
140. *See* Art. 9(2)(b) GDPR.
141. Schedule 1 Part 1 DPA 2018. *See also* below.
142. *See* Art. 9(2)(h) GDPR.
143. Schedule 1 Pt 1 para. 2 DPA 2018.
144. Section 11(1) of the DPA 2018.
145. Article 9(2)(i) of the UK GDPR.
146. Section 204(1) of the DPA 2018 lists the categories of health professionals.
147. Schedule 1 Pt 1 para. 3 DPA 2018.

9(2)(j) of the UK GDPR, special categories of data may be processed for archiving purposes, scientific or historical research purposes or statistical purposes. The DPA clarifies that this condition is met if the processing (a) is necessary for archiving purposes, scientific or historical research purposes or statistical purposes, (b) is carried out in accordance with Article 89(1) of the GDPR (as supplemented by section 19 of the DPA 2018), and (c) is in the public interest.[148]

75. Finally, Article 9(2)(g) of the UK GDPR which allows for the processing of special categories of data for reasons of substantial public interest, is complemented by Schedule 1 Part 2 of the DPA 2018. This provides an exhaustive but long list of purposes that can be considered as of substantial public interest and sets out specific additional conditions for processing for each of these areas. The areas mentioned in Schedule 1 Part 2 of the DPA 2018 are the following: statutory and government purposes; administration of justice and parliamentary purposes; equality of opportunity or treatment; racial and ethnic diversity at senior levels of organisations; preventing or detecting unlawful acts; protecting the public against dishonesty; regulatory requirements relating to unlawful acts and dishonesty; journalism in connection with unlawful acts and dishonesty; preventing fraud; suspicion of terrorist financing or money laundering; support for individuals with a particular disability or medical condition; counselling; safeguarding of children and individuals at risk; safeguarding of economic well-being of certain individuals; insurance; occupational pensions;[149] political parties; elected representatives responding to requests;[150] disclosure to elected representatives; informing elected representatives about prisoners; publication of legal judgments; anti-doping in sport; and standards of behaviour in sport.

76. It should be noted that some of the above purposes permit processing of only specified categories of special data (and not all types of special data). For instance, under the equality of opportunity and treatment purpose, processing is allowed 'when necessary for the purposes of identifying or keeping under review the existence or absence of equality of opportunity or treatment between groups of people specified in relation to that category with a view to enabling such equality to be promoted or maintained'.[151] The specified data that may be processed for this purpose are personal data revealing racial or ethnic origin, religious or philosophical beliefs, data concerning health and personal data concerning an individual's sexual orientation, but not other special personal data categories. Similarly, for the purpose of racial and ethnic diversity at senior levels of organisations, only personal data revealing racial or ethnic origin may be processed.[152] Moreover, processing of special categories of data for each of these purposes is subject to specific requirements

148. Schedule 1 Pt 1 para. 4 DPA 2018.
149. This processing condition can only be used if the data subject in question is a sibling, parent, grandparent, or great-grandparent of the scheme member. *See* Sch. 1 Pt 2 para. 21 DPA 2018.
150. This processing condition can only be used if the controller is the elected representative or is acting under their authority. *See* Sch. 1 Pt 2 para. 23 DPA 2018.
151. Schedule 1 Pt 2 para. 8 DPA 2018.
152. Schedule 1 Pt 2 para. 9 DPA 2018.

and safeguards. For example, processing for the purpose of racial and ethnic diversity at senior levels of organisations is permitted if carried out as part of a process of identifying suitable individuals to hold senior positions, is necessary to promote racial and ethnic diversity, can reasonably be carried out without the consent of the data subject and is not likely to cause substantial damage or substantial distress to an individual.[153]

77. Under the DPA 2018, controllers are required to have an 'appropriate policy document' in place when they carry out processing of special categories of personal data for reasons of substantial public interest.[154] The 'appropriate policy document' must explain the controller's procedures for securing compliance with the principles relating to the processing of personal data under Article 5 of the UK GDPR and outline the controller's policies as regards the retention and erasure of personal data processed in reliance on the applicable condition, giving an indication of how long such personal data is likely to be retained.[155] Controllers must review and update the document as appropriate, keep it for six months after processing is finished and make it available to the Information Commissioner on request.[156] The appropriate policy document must be accompanied by an additional safeguard: a record of processing under Article 30 of the UK GDPR which must include information on the condition relied on for processing; how the processing satisfies Article 6 of the UK GDPR (lawfulness of processing), and whether data is retained and erased in accordance with the policies and, if it is not, the reasons for not following those policies.[157]

78. Insofar as the processing of personal data relating to criminal convictions and offences is concerned, Article 10 of the UK GDPR is identical to Article 10 of the GDPR.[158] The processing of personal data relating to criminal convictions and offences is allowed only under the control of official authority or when it is authorised by the law providing for appropriate safeguards for the rights and freedoms of data subjects. Where the processing of data relating to criminal convictions and offences is not carried out under the control of official authority, the DPA 2018 provides that such processing can take place only for the specific purposes set out in Parts 1, 2 and 3 of Schedule 1.[159] Finally, the DPA 2018 sets out additional conditions for which criminal convictions data may be processed. These correspond to the legal grounds for processing of sensitive data in Article 9(2) of the UK GDPR (consent of the data subject, protecting individual's vital interests, processing by not-for-profit bodies, personal data in the public domain, legal claims, judicial acts,

---

153. *Ibid.*
154. Schedule 1 Pt 4 para. 38 DPA 2018. This requirement implements Art. 9(2)(g) GDPR which mandates that 'suitable and specific measures to safeguard the fundamental rights and the interests of the data subject' are adopted.
155. Schedule 1 Pt 4 para. 39 DPA 2018.
156. Schedule 1 Pt 4 para. 40 DPA 2018.
157. Schedule 1 Pt 4 para. 41 DPA 2018.
158. *See* Art. 10 GDPR.
159. Section 10(5) of the DPA 2018.

administration of accounts used in commission of indecency offences involving children, substantial public interest, etc.).[160]

79. It should be noted that the processing on a large scale of special categories of personal data and of data relating to criminal convictions and offences is also subject to a Data Protection Impact Assessment (DPIA).[161] Finally, a controller or processor must designate a data protection officer (DPO) where their core activities consist of processing special categories of data or data relating to criminal convictions on a large scale.[162]

160. Schedule 1 Pt 3 DPA 2018.
161. Article 35 of the UK GDPR.
162. Article 37 of the UK GDPR.

Part IV. Data Subject Rights

Chapter 1. Right to Be Informed

80. The UK GDPR grants individuals the same rights to be informed as the ones enshrined in Articles 13 and 14 of the EU GDPR. This is a 'key transparency requirement'[163] under EU law that is incorporated into the UK legal order. More particularly, Article 13 of the UK GDPR provides – without any material modifications to Article 13 of the EU GDPR – that where the controller collects personal data directly from the data subject, the controller must provide the data subject with specific information. This information includes:

(a) the identity and contact details of the controller and, where applicable, of the controller's representative;
(b) the contact details of the DPO, where applicable;
(c) the purposes of the processing for which the personal data are intended as well as the legal basis for the processing;
(d) where the processing is based on point (f) of Article 6(1), the legitimate interests pursued by the controller or by a third party;
(e) the recipients or categories of recipients of the personal data, if any;
(f) where applicable, the fact that the controller intends to transfer personal data to a third country or international organisation and the existence or absence of an adequacy decision under the DPA 2018.

81. Article 13(2) of the UK GDPR requires, in addition to the one mentioned in paragraph 1, further information should be provided to the data subject by the controller to ensure fair and transparent processing. This information includes:

(a) the period for which the personal data will be stored, or if that is not possible, the criteria used to determine that period;
(b) the existence of the right to request from the controller access to and rectification or erasure of personal data or restriction of processing concerning the data subject or to object to processing as well as the right to data portability;
(c) where the processing is based on consent, the existence of the right to withdraw consent at any time, without affecting the lawfulness of processing based on consent before its withdrawal;

163. *See* ICO, Guide to the GDPR, 92.

(d) the right to lodge a complaint with a supervisory authority;
(e) whether the provision of personal data is a statutory or contractual requirement, or a requirement necessary to enter into a contract, as well as whether the data subject is obliged to provide the personal data and of the possible consequences of failure to provide such data;
(f) the existence of automated decision-making, including profiling, and, at least in those cases, meaningful information about the logic involved, as well as the significance and the envisaged consequences of such processing for the data subject.[164]

82. The controller must take reasonable steps to ensure that any information provided to the data subject is given in a concise, intelligible and easily accessible form, using clear and plain language.[165] The information may be provided in any form, including electronic form, but the controller must ensure to provide the information in the same form as the request where it is practicable to do so.[166] Where the controller has reasonable doubts about the identity of an individual making a request,[167] the controller may request the provision of additional information to enable the controller to confirm the identity, and delay dealing with the request until the identity is confirmed.[168] Any information provided to data subjects must be provided free of charge.[169] However, where a request from a data subject is manifestly unfounded or excessive, the controller may charge a 'reasonable fee' for dealing with the request or refuse to act on the request.[170]

83. The ICO provides extensive guidance to controllers on the right to be informed.[171] It recognises that 'one of the biggest challenges is to encourage people to read privacy information. People are often unwilling to engage with detailed explanations, particularly where they are embedded in lengthy terms and conditions'.[172] However, according to the ICO, this does not mean that providing privacy information is a mere formality. It advises that the right to information should not necessarily be restricted to the delivery of a mere 'privacy notice' on a controller's website. Privacy information can be delivered in a range of ways, including: orally; in writing, on printed media and forms; through signage (an information poster in a public area); or electronically (text messages, on websites, in emails, in mobile

164. *See* analysis below.
165. Section 52 of DPA 2018. *See also* ICO, Guide to the GDPR, 94.
166. Section 52 of DPA 2018.
167. *See also* Art. 12(2) GDPR and UK GDPR.
168. Section 52 of DPA 2018.
169. Section 52 of DPA 2018.
170. Section 53 of DPA 2018.
171. *See* https://ico.org.uk/for-organisations/guide-to-data-protection/guide-to-the-general-data-protection-regulation-gdpr/the-right-to-be-informed/.
172. *See* https://ico.org.uk/for-organisations/guide-to-data-protection/guide-to-the-general-data-protection-regulation-gdpr/the-right-to-be-informed/how-should-we-draft-our-privacy-information/.

apps).[173] This information can be provided using a number of different techniques: a layered approach; dashboards; just-in-time notices; icons;[174] and mobile and smart device functionalities.[175]

84. The provision of Article 14 of the GDPR is also retained in the UK GDPR unchanged. Article 14 of the UK GDPR requires that the controller provides information to the data subject where personal data have not been obtained from the data subject.[176]

85. Articles 13 and 14 of the UK GDPR are subject to a number of exceptions. These implement Article 23 of the GDPR which allows for restrictions to the data subjects' rights. The exceptions to the data subject rights are found in Schedules 2–4 to the DPA 2018.

---

173. *See* https://ico.org.uk/for-organisations/guide-to-data-protection/guide-to-the-general-data-protection-regulation-gdpr/the-right-to-be-informed/what-methods-can-we-use-to-provide-privacy-information/.
174. *See also* Art. 12(7) of the UK GDPR and the EU GDPR.
175. *Ibid.*
176. The references to EU or Member State law included in Arts 14(5)(c)-(d) GDPR have been replaced with a reference to UK domestic law.

Chapter 2. Right of Access

86. The data subject's right of access is enshrined in Article 15 of the UK GDPR which retains the provision of Article 15 of the GDPR. According to this, the data subject has the right to obtain from the controller confirmation as to whether or not personal data concerning them are being processed and access to the personal data. The ICO has issued detailed guidance on the right to access (the ICO's 'Subject Access Request' – SAR Guidance).[177] Individuals have the right to receive the following information from controllers:

(a) the purposes for processing;
(b) the categories of personal data processed;
(c) the recipients or categories of recipient to whom the personal data have been or will be disclosed (including recipients in third countries);
(d) the data retention period or, where this is not possible, the criteria for determining how long it will be stored;
(e) the existence of an individual's right to request rectification, erasure or restriction or to object to processing;
(f) the right to lodge a complaint with the ICO;
(g) information about the source of the data, if this was not obtained directly from the individual;
(h) the existence of automated decision-making (including profiling) and information about the logic involved, as well as the significance and envisaged consequences of the processing for the individual;

87. Under the UK GDPR a subject access request can be made verbally, in writing (by letter) or electronically (e.g., by email or social media).[178] Access requests can be directed to any part of the controller's organisation and not a specific person or contact point. According to ICO's SAR Guide, a request might mistakenly state that it is a FOI request. However, if, in fact, it relates to the requester's personal data, the controller must treat it as a SAR.[179] Controllers must comply with a SAR without undue delay and at the latest within one month of receipt of the request.[180] Under the DPA 1998, controllers could charge a GBP 10 fee for a data subject request. This has now been abolished and under the current regime, a 'reasonable fee' for the administrative costs of complying with a request can be charged if the

177. *See* ICO's SAR Guide https://ico.org.uk/media/for-organisations/documents/2619803/right-of-access-1-0-20210520.pdf.
178. *Ibid.*
179. *Ibid.*
180. *Ibid.* This time period can be extended if the request is complex or where the controller has received a number of requests from the individual, for instance, a SAR, a request for erasure and a request for data portability simultaneously.

request is manifestly unfounded or excessive (merely repeats the substance of previous requests);[181] or an individual requests further copies of their data.[182] If the request is manifestly unfounded or excessive, the controller can also refuse to comply with a subject's access request.[183]

88. The data subject can make a complaint to the ICO if a controller fails to comply with a data subject request. Individuals can also bring a case against a controller before the courts, and they can seek compensation if they have suffered damage or distress because of a failure of the controller to comply with a SAR.

89. The data subject's right to access under Article 15 of the UK GDPR is subject to a number of exceptions. These implement Article 23 of the GDPR which allows for restrictions to the data subjects' rights. The exceptions to the data subject rights are found in Schedules 2–4 to the DPA 2018.

181. Section 53(1) of the DPA 2018.
182. Article 15(3) of the UK GDPR.
183. Section 53(1) of the DPA 2018.

Chapter 3. Rights of Rectification

90. The UK GDPR includes a right for individuals to have inaccurate personal data rectified, or in certain cases, completed if it is incomplete.[184] The DPA 2018 provides that personal data is inaccurate if it is incorrect or misleading as to any matter of fact.[185]

91. A request for rectification can be made verbally or in writing, and controllers normally have one calendar month to respond to this.[186] The ICO recommends that 'reasonable' steps should be taken by controllers to rectify personal data.[187] These steps depend on the nature of the personal data (inaccurate data must be rectified) and the purposes they will be used for (greater effort for rectification should be made for inaccurate data used to make significant decisions affecting individuals or others, rather than trivial ones).[188] If the request is manifestly unfounded or excessive, the controller can refuse to comply with a request for rectification.[189] In such cases, a fee for the administrative costs of complying with such requests can be charged.[190]

92. The data subject's right to rectification under Article 16 of the UK GDPR is subject to a number of exceptions. These implement Article 23 of the GDPR which allows for restrictions to the data subjects' rights. The exceptions to the data subject rights are found in Schedules 2–4 to the DPA 2018.

184. Article 16 of the UK GDPR. This is linked to the accuracy principle under Art. 5(1)(d) of the UK GDPR.
185. Section 205 of the DPA 2018.
186. ICO, Right to rectification https://ico.org.uk/for-organisations/guide-to-data-protection/guide-to-the-general-data-protection-regulation-gdpr/individual-rights/right-to-rectification/.
187. *Ibid.*
188. *Ibid.*
189. Section 53(1) of the DPA 2018.
190. Section 53(1) of the DPA 2018.

Chapter 4. Right to Erasure

93. The right to erasure ('right to be forgotten') is maintained without material changes in the UK GDPR.[191] This means that controllers are obliged to erase personal data without undue delay on the basis of the grounds under Article 17(1) of the UK GDPR, but the right to erasure does not apply if one of the reasons under Article 17(3) of the UK GDPR is applicable.

94. Controllers must respond to a request for erasure without undue delay and at the latest within one month, informing the data subject whether they have erased the data in question or their request has been refused. If the request is manifestly unfounded or excessive, the controller can refuse to comply with a request for erasure.[192] In such cases, a fee for the administrative costs of complying with such requests can be charged.[193]

95. The data subject's right to erasure under Article 17 of the UK GDPR is subject to a number of exceptions. These implement Article 23 of the GDPR which allows for restrictions to the data subjects' rights. The exceptions to the data subject rights are found in Schedules 2–4 to the DPA 2018.

191. Article 17 of the UK GDPR.
192. Section 53(1) of the DPA 2018.
193. Section 53(1) of the DPA 2018.

Chapter 5. Right to Restriction

96. With the exception of the words omitted in Article 18(2) to reflect the material scope of the UK GDPR there are no amendments of any significance to the EU GDPR.[194] Article 18 of the UK GDPR gives data subjects the right to restrict the processing of their personal data in specific circumstances. Unlike the specific right to object (Article 21 of the UK GDPR), the right to restricting the processing or use of personal data will arise where an issue arises in respect of: (i) the accuracy of the personal data being processed; (ii) processing is unlawful; (iii) where the purposes of the processing have ceased but are required by the data subject for the establishment, exercise or defence of legal claims; and (d) the data subject has objected to processing pursuant to Article 21(1) pending the verification whether the legitimate grounds of the controller override those of the data subject.

97. In situations where an individual exercises the right to restrict on the grounds of accuracy or the right to object to processing under Article 21(1), a data controller will be under an obligation to undertake steps to determine the accuracy (in the case of the former) or assess whether there are legitimate grounds to override the right of the data subject (in the case of the latter). It is worth recalling, the right to restriction applies to any type of processing operation involving the data subject's personal data or data held by the controller, as set out in Article 4 of the UK GDPR. The definition of 'processing' is sufficiently wide and will include 'any operation or set of operations which is performed on personal data or on sets of personal data, whether or not by automated means'.[195] The data subject can exercise the right to the collection, recording, transmission or adaptation of his personal data.[196] In the event that the data subject is successful, the controller marks the stored personal data with the aim of limiting their processing in the future.[197] This is likely to be relevant where the personal data is processed by automated filing systems. Where the processing operation takes place within a large organisation or business, controllers will need to ensure that they have adopted technical or similar measures that highlight the fact that the processing is restricted. Furthermore, the relevant personal data, with the exception of storage can only be processed if the data subject consents, for the establishment, exercise or defence of legal claims, for the protection of the rights of another natural or legal person or where there are public interest grounds.[198] It should be apparent from the foregoing that when the right to restriction is exercised, the data subject identifies the personal data concerned and specific circumstances as well as the restriction envisaged. For example, a data subject may wish for his personal data to be temporarily made unavailable to the public

194. *See* Words in Art. 18(2) omitted (31.12.2020) by virtue of The Data Protection, Privacy and Electronic Communications (Amendments etc) (EU Exit) Regulations 2019 (S.I. 2019/419), reg. 1(2), Sch. 1 para. 16 (with reg. 5, Sch. 1 para. 80); 2020 c. 1, Sch. 5 para. 1(1).
195. Article 4(2) of the UK GDPR.
196. Article 4(3) of the UK GDPR.
197. Article 4(3) of the UK GDPR.
198. Article 18(2). *See* The Data Protection, Privacy and Electronic Communications (Amendments etc) (EU Exit) Regulations 2019 (S.I. 2019/419), reg. 1(2), Sch. 1 para. 16 (with reg. 5, Sch. 1 para. 80); 2020 c. 1, Sch. 5 para. 1(1).

or users.[199] The Information Commissioner has provided extensive guidance on procedural and oversight mechanisms that controllers need to put in place when data subjects make an application to have the processing of personal data restricted.[200] For example, a controller can refuse to comply with a request to have processing of personal data restricted if the ground relied upon is shown to be manifestly unfounded; or excessive. The Information Commissioner advises controllers not to have a blanket policy but make assessments on a case-by-case basis. When it is determined that the request is manifestly unfounded or excessive clear reasons must be provided for the decision within one month of receipt. Examples of requests to restrict which come within this category would be instances of malicious intent to harass organisations or cause significant disruption. The fact that the request is unfounded is not sufficient to permit rejection. The inclusion of the word 'manifestly' means that a much higher threshold must be met. The controller is also under an obligation to inform data subjects of their right to make a complaint to the ICO or another supervisory authority; and their ability to seek to enforce this right through a judicial remedy. The UK GDPR does not specify how to make a valid request. Therefore, an individual can make a request for restriction verbally or in any other reasonable form of communication (e.g., phone call, email or letter). The Information Commissioner has also advised controllers to adopt good practice by ensuring that there is a policy setting out the mechanisms for dealing with requests and communication of decisions. In some cases, given the time and costs incurred in dealing with the administration of requests, a 'reasonable fee' for the administrative costs of complying with the request if it is manifestly unfounded or excessive can be charged.

199. *See* Recital 67 GDPR.
200. *See* https://ico.org.uk/for-organisations/guide-to-data-protection/guide-to-the-general-data-protection-regulation-gdpr/individual-rights/right-to-restrict-processing/.

Chapter 6. Profiling

98. Article 22(1) of the UK GDPR seems to continue very much in line with the EU GDPR approach to the use of automated decision-making processes (including profiling):

> The data subject shall have the right not to be subject to a decision based solely on automated processing, including profiling, which produces legal effects concerning him or her or similarly significantly affects him or her.

99. The Information Commissioner has provided detailed guidance on terms such as 'decision based solely', 'produce legal effects' and 'significantly affects'.[201] These complement those provided by the EDPB. The definition of 'profiling' in Article 4(4) of the UK GDPR is retained. There is unlikely to be much way of difference in understanding what constitutes 'profiling'.[202] For example, whether a processing operation constitutes 'profiling' will be dependent on all three elements being present: automated processing; processing of personal data; and evaluation of personal traits relating to a natural person. The fact that the first or third elements are not present does not mean that other obligations imposed on controllers under the UK GDPR will not be present. A brief comment will be offered in respect of the three elements that constitute 'profiling'.

§1. Any Form of Automated Processing

100. Article 4(4) of the UK GDPR targets automated processing operations and systems, with the continued focus on the problems of opacity, accuracy and explainability. Care needs to be taken to not readily assume that the mere fact of using an automated process does not necessarily mean that profiling has taken place. Consider, for example, a motorist issued with a traffic violation fine. The CCTV camera records the vehicle identification number and the issue of a fine can be regarded as the result of an automated decision-making process. This would not be regarded as profiling since other elements in Article 4(4) of the UK GDPR need to be present. If, however, additional factors are taken into account, which involves combining other data relating to the individual, such as personal traits of the individual or existence of prior traffic regulation violations, this would constitute 'profiling'.

---

201. *See* Information Commissioner, Guide automated decision making and profiling https://ico.org.uk/for-organisations/guide-to-data-protection/guide-to-the-general-data-protection-regulation-gdpr/automated-decision-making-and-profiling/ and Big Data and Data Protection and Big Data, Artificial Intelligence, machine learning and data protection: https://ico.org.uk/media/for-organisations/documents/2013559/big-data-ai-ml-and-data-protection.pdf.
202. Article 4(4) of the UK GDPR.

§2. Involves Processing of Personal Data

101. Data protection rules do not come into operation until personal data is processed. The rationale and much of the policy and academic commentary surrounding profiling revolves around the process and consequences for individuals, when knowledge and insights about individuals are generated through the use of machine learning techniques. As knowledge is generated from the use of diverse digital tools and services (e.g., volunteered data, location and traffic data and inferred data), the broad definition of profiling will require controllers to undertake impact assessment measures where appropriate. The fact that personal data can now be combined with other forms of non-personal data illustrates the importance of regulating risks associated with profiling and automated decision-making more broadly by engaging with other UK GDPR provisions for promoting transparency, fairness and accountability. For example, inferring an individual's health from records of the type of foods consumed would be regarded as 'profiling'. It is profiling if the data is used to draw correlations or even base predictions by combining non-personal data. Furthermore, interactions with mobile phones or apps as well as visiting websites enable digital traces to be combined with online identifiers such as IP addresses or cookie identifiers to create profiles of individuals.[203]

§3. Used to Evaluate Personal Aspects Relating to a Natural Person

102. The final element in the definition of profiling is the identification of the scope and limits to using forms of automated decision-making that involve reaching decisions about the individual, making predictions or creating a profile based on the person's performance at work, economic situation, health, personal preferences, interests, reliability, behaviour, location or movements. There mere fact personal data is processed will not be sufficient for the operation to be regarded as profiling. Any determination of whether profiling is involved needs to be guided by the aims of the automated processing of personal data. For example, cookies and similar technologies are used to track individuals on the internet with the aim of taking decisions about targeting them with advertisements, or to analyse their personal preferences, behaviours or attitudes.[204]

103. Automated decision-making and the increasing use of profiling, in the age of AI, machine learning and big data, continue to raise important questions on the optimal approach to balancing data subject's rights with other equally legitimate interests and freedoms.[205] The EU GDPR provides a framework to help resolve this dilemma through its provisions in Article 22(2), (3) and (4). The approach adopted

203. Recital 30 UK GDPR.
204. Recital 24 UK GDPR.
205. *See* ICO, AI and Data Protection Risk Toolkit v1.0 https://ico.org.uk/for-organisations/guide-to-data-protection/key-dp-themes/guidance-on-ai-and-data-protection/ai-and-data-protection-risk-toolkit/.

by the UK GDPR raises some interesting questions about whether there is a trend towards moving away from the safeguards and values embedded in the Charter of Fundamental Rights.

104. There is no substantive difference between the UK GDPR and EU GDPR with regard to contractual necessity or data subject's explicit consent as permitting automated decision-making.[206] Article 22(3) of the UK GDPR provides that in the cases referred to in points (a) and (c) of paragraph 2, the data controller shall implement suitable measures to safeguard the data subject's rights and freedoms and legitimate interests, at least the right to obtain human intervention on the part of the controller, to express his or her point of view and to contest the decision. Recital 71 provides further clarification with regard to the transparency, fairness and accountability obligations owed by controllers to data subjects. Controllers need to provide specific information regarding the use of automated decision-making, make clear the data subject's right to obtain human intervention, ensure that an opportunity is made available for views to be expressed, and provide an explanation of the decision reached. The safeguards also include the right to challenge the decision and that such processes should not concern a child. Article 22(3) of the EU GDPR permits automated decision-making if authorised by Member State law. Article 22(2) of the UK GDPR controllers can use automated decision-making if required or authorised by domestic law but on condition that suitable measures are put in place to safeguard the data subject's rights and freedoms and legitimate interests. Irrespective of which ground is relied upon in Article 22(2) of the UK GDPR, automated decision-making is not to be based on special categories of personal data referred to in Article 9(1), unless point (a) or (g) of Article 9(2) applies and suitable measures to safeguard the data subject's rights and freedoms and legitimate interests are in place. However, the DPA 2018 introduces some provisions that will have a bearing on how Article 9(2)(g). Additionally, under Article 23A of the UK GDPR, section 14 of the DPA 2018 section 14 of the 2018 Act, enables provisions to be made with regard to safeguarding data subjects' rights, freedoms and legitimate interests in cases that come within Article 22(2)(b) of the UK GDPR. With regard to Article 9(2)(g) of the UK GDPR, section 10(3) of the DPA 2018 processing must satisfy one of the conditions set out in Part 2 Schedule 1. The conditions set out in Part 2 Schedule 1 include statutory or government purposes, preventing or detecting unlawful acts, support for individuals with a disability or medical condition, political parties, protecting the public against dishonesty and administration of justice and parliamentary purposes. Section 14 of the DPA 2018 makes provision for 'significant decisions' when automated decision-making is to be authorised by law under Article 22(2)(b) of the UK GDPR. A 'significant decision' under section 14(2) of the DPA 2018 mirrors the EU GDPR. An automated decision-making operation will be a 'qualifying significant decision', and where section 14 applies, controllers will need to meet the requirements for transparency, fairness and accountability.[207] For example, the local authority or organisation must notify the data subject in writing as soon as reasonably practicable, that a decision has been taken based solely on

206. Article 22 (a) and (c) of the UK GDPR.
207. Section 14 (4), (5) and (6).

automated processing, and time period within which responses or requests are to be received.[208] The Secretary of State may by regulations make such further provision considered appropriate to provide suitable measures to safeguard a data subject's rights, freedoms and legitimate interests in connection with the taking of qualifying significant decisions based solely on automated processing.[209] The regulations introduced by the Secretary of State in pursuance of section 14(7) of the DPA 2018 will be subject to the affirmative procedure.

105. With regard to the use of automated decision-making by law enforcement, safeguarding provisions are set out in DPA 2018 Part 3 sections 49 and 50. Section 49 (2) treats a significant decision as one producing an 'adverse' legal effect but not if the outcome is positive.[210] This seems to be a type of ex post facto rationalisation, and the inclusion of the adjective is not really helpful. Automated decision-making by intelligence services is covered by Part 4 sections 96–98 of the DPA 2018.[211]

---

208. Section 14(4) of the DPA 2018.
209. Section 14(7) of the DPA 2018.
210. *See* the role of the Information Commissioner with regards to rights arising from Law Enforcement processing under Part 3 – s. 51 of the DPA 2018.
211. Note specifically s. 98(1) of the DPA 2018 the right to require information about the reasoning underlying the decision reached through automated decision-making.

Chapter 7. Right to Object

106. With the exception to the words omitted by the DPPEC Regulations in Article 21(5) of the UK GDPR, the right to object to processing generally is very much in keeping with the scope and nature of the rights set out in the EU GDPR. The data subject can assert the right to object to the processing of his or her personal data if the legal basis for processing relied upon by the controller is founded on Article 6(1) (e) or (f). The right can also be asserted if personal data is used to profile the data subject. Once the right to object is asserted, processing will cease unless the controller demonstrates compelling legitimate grounds for the processing which override the interests, rights and freedoms of the data subject or for the establishment, exercise or defence of legal claims.[212] In respect of processing of personal data for direct marketing purposes, the data subject shall have the right to object at any time to processing of personal data concerning him or her for such marketing, which includes profiling to the extent that it is related to such direct marketing.[213] The right to object to processing of personal data is not absolute. For example, if the personal data is processed for scientific or historical research purposes or statistical purposes pursuant to Article 89(1) of the UK GDPR, the right to object will not take precedence in cases where the processing is necessary for the performance of a task carried out for reasons of public interest.[214] Finally, Article 21(5) of the UK GDPR provides that the right to object by automated means using technical specifications in the context of information society services, notwithstanding domestic law made before IP completion day implementing Directive 2002/58/EC of the European Parliament and of the Council of 12 July 2002 concerning the processing of personal data and the protection of privacy in the electronic communications sector.

107. Article 21 of the UK GDPR has an equivalent right in paragraph 8 Part 2 Schedule 1 DPA 2018. Schedule 1 DPA 2018 deals with, amongst other things, special categories of personal data. Paragraph 8(3) to (5) Part 2 envisages that an individual affected by the process of identification or monitoring for equality of opportunity may serve notice in writing to the controller requiring the latter not to process personal data in respect of which the individual is the data subject (and has not given notice in writing withdrawing that requirement).[215]

108. Another example of the right to object under the DPA 2018 relates to processing of personal data by intelligence services. Section 99(1) states that the right to object can be asserted on the ground that, for specified reasons relating to the situation of the data subject, the processing in question constitutes an unwarranted interference with the interests or rights of the data subject. The data subject concerned can assert the right at any time by serving notice on the controller, stipulating that

212. *See* reasoning in *AEDP (Costeja) v. Google Spain* C-131/12. Equivalent approaches can also be seen in *NT1 & NT2 v. Google LLC* [2018] EWHC 799.
213. Article 21(2) of the UK GDPR.
214. Article 21(6) of the UK GDPR.
215. Paragraph 8 (5) Part 2 Sch. 1 DPA 2018.

the personal data relating to the data subject is not processed or that the processing for a specified purpose or in a specified manner is to cease. The controller is given twenty-one days to respond, indicating compliance with the request or indicating that the relevant grounds relied upon by the data subject are not well founded.[216]

216. Section 99 (3) of the DPA 2018. On application to the court and orders *see* s. 99(4), (7) and (5) of the DPA 2018.

Part V. Duties of Controllers and Processors

Chapter 1. National Rules Regarding Duties of Controllers

109. As noted previously, following the UK's departure from the EU, reference will now need to be made to the UK's data protection framework for determining the allocation and distribution of responsibilities owed by those who process personal data. To identify which obligations apply to controllers and joint controllers, one has to determine whether the meaning ascribed by Article 4(7) of the UK GDPR continues to apply or it is replaced by DPA 2018 provisions. Section 6 of the DPA 2018 provides an additional set of provisions that complement the definition of 'controller' provided by Article 4(7) of the UK GDPR.

110. While the term 'data controller' has been commonly associated with the obligations assumed by any person processing personal data, both the UK GDPR and DPA 2018 use the term 'controller' to ascribe the role and responsibilities set out in the definition provided in Article 4(7) of the UK GDPR.[217] Article 4(7) of the UK GDPR defines a controller as comprising natural or legal persons, public authority, agency or other body which, alone or jointly with others, determines the purposes and means of the processing of personal data.

111. There are four key elements to be noted in the definition of a controller: (i) natural or legal persons, (ii) overall control over the purposes and means, (iii) can be undertaken alone or jointly; and (iv) and processing of personal data. Like the EU GDPR, a controller can be a natural person or legal entity, such as a business or corporation. For a person or legal entity to be characterised as a controller, it must be shown to have determined both the purposes and means for processing personal data. In the leading case of *Bodil v. Lindqvist*, it was held that an individual posting information about certain parish activities could be regarded as a controller.[218] It did not matter that the means of processing was made possible by an information society services provider. The crucial issue here seems to be the overall control in deciding what information is to be processed. In *Google Spain v. Costeja*, it was held that the global technology corporation was a controller as it had overall control over the display of the search results.[219] However, Article 2(2)(a) of the UK GDPR states

217. This definition of a controller is subject to s. 6 of the DPA 2018. *See* later discussion.
218. Case C-101/01, Criminal proceedings against Bodil Lindqvist, 6 Nov. 2003.
219. C-131/2, *Google Spain SL, Google Inc. v. Agencia Española de Protección de Datos, Mario Costeja González*.

that the individuals will not be regarded as a controller, if the processing of personal data is undertaken in the course of a purely personal or household activity.[220]

112. The distinction between the controller and processor has been the subject of judicial and policy commentary.[221] In *Google Spain*, the fact that the specific processing operation was undertaken separately did not absolve the search engine provider from its responsibilities as a controller, as it had overall control over the purposes and means by which search results were displayed. The Information Commissioner has indicated that even where an organisation does not have a separate legal personality – as in the case of unincorporated associations such as sports clubs or voluntary groups, the controller is under an obligation to establish a point of contact, setting out the responsibilities of those in the organisation who are likely to act as the controller or joint controllers. From a data protection perspective, such an organisation could designate the organisation as a whole as the controller, but a preferable course would be to stipulate which members are instrumental in making decisions about the processing by the organisation.[222] This broad definition of the controller is subject to section 6 of the DPA 2018. Section 6(2) states that those who are required by an enactment to process personal data for specified purposes will also be treated as a controller. Section 209 and 201 also designate those who are treated as controllers. Finally, sections 32(1) and (2) and 83(1) and (2) set out the requirements for controllership under Parts 3 and 4 of the DPA 2018 respectively.

§1. The Crown and Parliament

113. For the purposes of the UK GDPR and the DPA 2018, each government department is to be treated as a person separate from the other government departments (to the extent that is not already the case).[223] In cases where government departments are unable to enter into contracts with each other, a provision of the GDPR or this act that would require relations between them to be governed by a contract (or other binding legal act) in writing is to be treated as satisfied if the relations governed by a memorandum of understanding (MoU). Section 210 states that Parts 1, 2 and 5 to 7 of the DPA 2018 apply to the processing of personal data by or on behalf of either House of Parliament. The controller in respect of that data for the purposes of the GDPR and this Act is the Corporate Officer of that House.

220. Article 2(2)(c) of the UK GDPR.
221. *See*, for example, C-131/2, *Google Spain SL, Google Inc. v. Agencia Española de Protección de Datos, Mario Costeja González*, C-210/16 – Wirtschaftsakademie Schleswig-Holstein and EDPS Guidelines on the concepts of controller, processor and joint controllership under Regulation (EU) 2018/1725, 7 Nov. 2019.
222. Article 4(7) of the UK GDPR.
223. Section 209(2) of the DPA 2018.

§2. Law Enforcement and Intelligence Services

114. Section 32(1) of the DPA 2018 defines a 'controller' as a competent authority which, alone or jointly with others, determines the purposes and means of the processing of personal data or is regarded as a controller by virtue of processing personal data for the for purposes for which it is required by an enactment to be processed, and by means by which it is required by an enactment to be processed.[224] The definition of a controller mirrors those of law enforcement.[225]

224. Section 32(2). *See also* s. 6(2) of the DPA 2018.
225. Section 83(1) and (2).

Chapter 2. National Rules Regarding Joint Controllers

115. An important question that arises when personal data is processed is whether the entity concerned has, either alone or jointly with others, determined the purposes and means of the processing of personal data.[226] The notion of determining the purposes and means of personal data should be particularly difficult to ascertain. It does not matter if the controller does not exercise authority over every single step in the processing operation. It suffices if the controller can be said to exercise ultimate control or authority to determine whether personal data should be processed. In Case C-131/12, *Google Spain v. gencia Española de Protección de Datos (AEPD), Mario Costeja González,* the CJEU decision to adopt an expansive view of the controller was in large part influenced by the need to provide data subjects with complete protection to their fundamental freedoms and rights:[227]

> Inasmuch as the activity of a search engine is therefore liable to affect significantly, and additionally compared with that of the publishers of websites, the fundamental rights to privacy and to the protection of personal data, the operator of the search engine as the person determining the purposes and means of that activity must ensure, within the framework of its responsibilities, powers and capabilities, that the activity meets the requirements of Directive 95/46 in order that the guarantees laid down by the directive may have full effect and that effective and complete protection of data subjects, in particular of their right to privacy, may actually be achieved.

116. There are no material changes to the determination of a joint controllership in existence or the scope and nature of responsibilities owed by joint controllers. Article 26 of the UK GDPR states that where two or more controllers jointly determine the purposes and means of processing, they shall be joint controllers. To ensure clarity of the respective responsibilities for compliance with the obligations under data protection law, in particular, as regards the exercising of the rights of the data subject and their respective duties to provide the information referred to in Articles 13 and 14, joint controllers are under an obligation to determine how these obligations are to be fulfilled.[228] The Information Commissioner provides a checklist of features in the relationship that gives rise to joint controllership. These are the existence of a common objective with regard to processing, the existence of similar or identical purposes for processing the personal data, the personal data being processed (personal data from a defined database), the process being designed together with the collaboration of another, the existence if any of a policy governing processing and management of information rules. The determination of whether

226. Article 4(7).
227. Google Spain and Google, C-131/12, EU:C:2014:317, paragraph 38.
228. Words in Art. 26(1) substituted (31.12.2020) by The Data Protection, Privacy and Electronic Communications (Amendments etc) (EU Exit) Regulations 2019 (S.I. 2019/419), reg. 1(2), Sch. 1 para. 20 (with reg. 5); 2020 c. 1, Sch. 5 para. 1(1).

a joint controller relationship exists is also relevant to determining issues about accountability and liability, when issues about enforcement and remedies are raised. To this end, the mischief of Article 26 is to ensure that data subjects have a point of contact.[229]

229. Article 26(3) of the UK GDPR and Recitals 36 and 81–84.

Chapter 3. National Rules with Regard to Processors

117. Historically, the current regulation applicable to processors is considered 'one of the biggest shifts'[230] from the DPA 1998. This is because the DPA 1998 applied to controllers but processors were not covered by any direct obligations. This has now been amended to reflect the rules of the GDPR.

118. Indeed, the definition of 'processor' under Article 4(8) of the UK GDPR and the rules regarding processors are identical to the ones of the GDPR.[231] Where processing is to be carried out on behalf of a controller, the controller should use only processors providing sufficient guarantees to implement appropriate technical and organisational measures in such a manner that processing meets the requirements of the UK GDPR and ensures the protection of the rights of the data subject.[232] Whenever a controller uses a processor, there must be a written contract (or other legal act) in place. The contract is important so that both parties understand their respective responsibilities and liabilities.[233] The contact should set out the subject-matter and duration of the processing, the nature and purpose of the processing, the type of personal data involved, the categories of data subjects and the obligations and rights of the controller.[234] Furthermore, the contract (or other legal act) should stipulate that the processor:

(a) processes data only on the controller's documented instructions;
(b) ensures that people processing data are subject to a duty of confidentiality;
(c) takes appropriate measures to ensure the security of processing;
(d) engages a sub-processor only with the controller's prior authorisation and under a written contract;
(e) takes appropriate measures to help the controller respond to requests from individuals exercising their data subject rights;
(f) assists the controller in complying with its UK GDPR obligations in relation to the security of processing, the notification of personal data breaches and DPIAs taking into account the nature of processing and the information available;
(g) deletes or returns all personal data to the controller after the end of the provision of services relating to processing;
(h) contributes to audits and inspections conducted by the controller or another auditor mandated by the controller.[235]

119. A processor can make their own day-to-day operational decisions, but they should only process personal data in line with a controller's instructions, unless it is

230. Louise Townsend in Jay, *supra*, 13, 445.
231. Article 4(8) GDPR, 'a natural or legal person, public authority, agency or other body which processes personal data on behalf of the controller'.
232. Article 28(1) of the UK GDPR.
233. ICO, Contracts and liabilities between controllers and processors https://ico.org.uk/for-organisations/guide-to-data-protection/guide-to-the-general-data-protection-regulation-gdpr/contracts-and-liabilities-between-controllers-and-processors-multi/.
234. *See* Art. 28(3) of the UK GDPR.
235. *Ibid.*

required to do otherwise by UK law (in that case they must inform the controller of this legal requirement before the processing, unless that law prohibits it doing so on important grounds of public interest).[236] If a processor acts outside of a controller's instructions and determines the purpose and means of processing, then they are to be considered a controller.[237]

120. Processors should maintain a record of all categories of processing activities carried out on behalf of a controller, containing: (a) the name and contact details of the processor or processors and of each controller on behalf of which the processor is acting, and, where applicable, of the controller's or the processor's representative, and the DPO; (b) the categories of processing carried out on behalf of each controller; (c) where applicable, transfers of personal data to a third country or an international organisation; (d) where possible, a general description of the technical and organisational security measures that they have adopted.[238] Processors must cooperate, on request, with the ICO in the performance of their tasks.[239]

121. In terms of enforcement, processors are subject to the investigative powers of the ICO and could be issued administrative fines or other penalties. Claims against processors can also be brought by individuals in courts. In particular, processors can be held liable to pay compensation for any damage caused by processing, including non-material damage such as distress.[240] Processors may only be held liable for the damage if: they have failed to comply with UK GDPR provisions specifically relating to processors; or they have acted without or against the controller's lawful instructions.[241] A processor shall be exempt from liability if it proves that it is not in any way responsible for the event giving rise to the damage.[242]

236. *See* Art. 29 of the UK GDPR.
237. *See* ICO, What responsibilities and liabilities do processors have in their own right? https://ico.org.uk/for-organisations/guide-to-data-protection/guide-to-the-general-data-protection-regulation-gdpr/contracts-and-liabilities-between-controllers-and-processors-multi/responsibilities-and-liabilities-for-processors-in-their-own-right/#1.
238. *See* Art. 30(2) of the UK GDPR.
239. *See* Art. 31 of the UK GDPR.
240. *See* Art. 82 of the UK GDPR. *See also* Art. 82(5) of the UK GDPR.
241. ICO, What responsibilities and liabilities do processors have in their own right?, *supra*, 137.
242. *See* Art. 82(3) of the UK GDPR.

Chapter 4. Security Obligations

122. The obligation to ensure the security of personal data in UK law is one of the data protection principles enshrined in Article 5(1)(f) of the UK GDPR.[243] Article 32 of the UK GDPR – which maintains Article 32 of the EU GDPR without any changes – sets out the technical and organisational measures that controllers and processors need to implement to ensure a level of security appropriate to the risk. Furthermore, Article 33 of the UK GDPR – which corresponds to Article 33 of the EU GDPR – requires the notification of personal data breach to the Information Commissioner and Article 34 of the UK GDPR – which corresponds to Article 34 of the GDPR – regulates the communication of a personal data breach likely to result in a high risk to the rights and freedoms of natural persons to the data subject.

123. The ICO has issued guidance on security obligations under the UK GDPR[244] and has developed, in collaboration with the National Cyber Security Centre (NCSC) a 'security outcomes' framework[245] as well as an 'Accountability Framework'.[246] It has also published detailed guidance on different aspects of IT security.[247]

124. The ICO has issued high fines for data breaches. In 2020, it fined British Airways GBP 20 million for a data breach affecting more than 400,000 of its customers[248] and issued a fine of GBP 18.4 million to Marriott International for personal data security failures.[249]

243. The 'integrity and confidentiality' principle.
244. ICO, Security https://ico.org.uk/for-organisations/guide-to-data-protection/guide-to-the-general-data-protection-regulation-gdpr/security/.
245. *See* ICO, Security outcomes https://ico.org.uk/for-organisations/security-outcomes/.
246. *See* ICO, Accountability Framework https://ico.org.uk/for-organisations/accountability-framework/.
247. *See* ICO, *supra* 145.
248. ICO fines British Airways GBP 20 million for data breach affecting more than 400,000 customers https://ico.org.uk/about-the-ico/news-and-events/news-and-blogs/2020/10/ico-fines-british-airways-20m-for-data-breach-affecting-more-than-400-000-customers.
249. ICO fines Marriott International Inc GBP 18.4 million for failing to keep customers' personal data secure https://ico.org.uk/about-the-ico/news-and-events/news-and-blogs/2020/10/ico-fines-marriott-international-inc-184million-for-failing-to-keep-customers-personal-data-secure/.

Chapter 5. Data Protection Officer or Similar Functions

125. The UK GDPR maintains, without any material changes, the provisions of the EU GDPR on the designation and tasks of DPOs.[250] Under the UK GDPR, controllers and processors must appoint a DPO where: (a) the processing is carried out by a public authority or body, except for courts acting in their judicial capacity; (b) the core activities of the controller or the processor consist of processing operations which, by virtue of their nature, their scope and/or their purposes, require regular and systematic monitoring of data subjects on a large scale; or (c) the core activities of the controller or the processor consist of processing on a large scale of special categories of data or data relating to criminal convictions and offences. Section 7 of DPA 2018 defines 'public authority' and 'public body' for the purposes of the UK GDPR. Furthermore, Part 3 of the DPA 2018, which regulates processing for law enforcement purposes, mandates that 'the controller must designate a data protection officer, unless the controller is a court, or other judicial authority, acting in its judicial capacity'.[251]

126. Under the UK GDPR, the DPO shall have the following tasks: (a) to inform and advise the controller or the processor of their obligations under the UK GDPR and other data protection laws; (b) to monitor compliance with the UK GDPR and with the policies of the controller or processor in relation to the protection of personal data, including the assignment of responsibilities, awareness-raising and training of staff involved in processing operations, and the related audits; (c) to advice and monitor impact assessments under Article 35 of the UK GDPR; (d) to cooperate with the ICO; (e) to act as the contact point for the ICO and individuals whose data are processed. The ICO cannot charge a fee for any service they provide to a DPO.[252] However, if the DPO's request to the ICO is 'manifestly unfounded or excessive', the ICO may charge a reasonable fee for dealing with the request or refuse to act on the request.[253]

250. Articles 37–39 of UK GDPR.
251. Section 69(1) of the DPA 2018.
252. Section 134 of the DPA 2018.
253. Section 135 of the DPA 2018.

Part VI. Codes of Conduct and Certification

127. Following the UK's departure from the EU, the framework governing the development of codes of conduct now comprises: (i) codes developed under the UK GDPR; and (ii) those created under the mandate of the UK DPA 2018.

128. Codes of conduct ('codes') are an increasingly popular instrument used to regulate the operations and activities undertaken by data controllers when processing personal data.[254]

129. There are two parallel regimes that need to be borne in mind. First, the power to create statutory codes under the DPA 2018.[255] Second, the established framework for codes and certification is provided by the UK GDPR.

§1. Statutory Codes under the DPA 2018

130. The Information Commissioner is under a duty to produce four statutory codes. These are: the data sharing code, the direct marketing code, the age-appropriate design code, and the data protection and journalism code.[256] The DPA 2018 also permits the Secretary of State to require the Information Commissioner to develop additional codes. These statutory codes must be laid before Parliament. The Secretary of State is required to submit the code to Parliament as soon as it is reasonably practicable.[257] The codes are subject to a negative resolution procedure. This means that the codes do not become effective until the expiry of the forty-day period, within which time either House has not resolved to reject the code.[258] The forty-day time period takes effect from the date when the code is laid before each

254. *See* s. 36(4) of the Data Protection Act 1984 and Directive 95/46/EC made provision for Member States to integrate national and EU codes (s. 51(3) to (5) of the DPA 1998). The framework provided by the GDPR will continue to be applied in the UK GDPR, with specific reference to the UK context. This chapter focuses on GDPR and UK GDPR codes but provides a brief coverage of codes under the DPA 2018.
255. Note that Codes of Conduct developed under the GDPR will require an independent supervisory authority.
256. Sections 121–124 of the DPA 2018. *See also* Part 5 of the DPA 2018.
257. Section 125 of the DPA 2018.
258. Section 125(4) of the DPA 2018.

House of Parliament.[259] If the code is opposed during the forty-day period, Information Commissioner is under an obligation to issue the code which comes into effect twenty-one days after approval.[260] The Information Commissioner will have to keep the code under review.

131. With regard to the legal status of statutory codes, these are not regarded as being legally binding.[261] However, codes are admissible as evidence in legal proceedings, and a court or tribunal is required to take account of its provisions.[262] The Information Commissioner can also take into account the provisions of the code to the extent that it is relevant to the question of compliance with data protection rules or obligations. To date, two codes have been developed: the age-appropriate design code and the data sharing code.

132. The age-appropriate design code (Children's code) was developed to establish new rules governing the collection and processing of children's personal data, specifically by those providing online services. The Information Commissioner was required to prepare a code which provides guidance on 'appropriate standards' for those information society services likely to be accessed by children. During the development phase, the Information Commissioner embarked on a wide consultation exercise, which included children, parents, child development experts, persons representing the interests of children and trade associations. The Children's code was laid before Parliament on 11 June 2020 and accompanied by the publication of an Explanatory Memorandum.[263] The Children's code came into force on 2 September 2020 with a transitional period of twelve months.[264]

133. Any service 'normally provided for remuneration, at a distance by electronic means and at the individual request of a recipient of services' will be within the scope of the Children's code. The services include those made available to children through the use of mobile applications; accessing social media platforms, online retailers, electronic communication services and tools, interactive games, toys and devices, and news and educational services. Counselling and preventative services are not covered by the Children's code.[265]

134. The guidance takes into account the fact that children have different needs at different ages, and the standards are child-focused in the sense that due regard must be given by those processing a child's personal data to the best interests of

259. Section 125(7) of the DPA 2018.
260. Section 125(4) of the DPA 2018.
261. Section 127(1) of the DPA 2018.
262. Section 127(2), (3) and (4).
263. *See* Department for Digital, Culture, Media and Sport: https://www.gov.uk/government/publications/explanatory-memorandum-to-the-age-appropriate-design-code-2020-2020/explanatory-memorandum-to-the-age-appropriate-design-code-2020-2020.
264. Section 123(1) of the DPA 2018.
265. Section 123(7) of the DPA 2018. Note that the Children's code does not apply in other instances, such as services not provided on a commercial basis, Intelligence Services, the exercise by law enforcement agencies of their powers under Part 3 of the DPA 2018.

children principle.[266] An 'age-appropriate design' will require information services providers to ensure that the services are 'appropriate for use by, and meet the developmental needs of, children.'[267]

135. Under the UK GDPR, the enforcement powers of the Commissioner extend to data controllers and data processors. It is not entirely clear as to the extent to which enforcement of the Children's code extends to these entities. It may very well be that providers of information society services will ensure that those providing software and design services have taken into account the standards in the code through the contractual terms of engagement. Given the global nature of information society services, reference should be made to the likely territorial reach of the Children's code. Article 3(2) of the UK GDPR states that data controllers and data processors based outside the UK will be subject to the Children's code if they offer goods or services to data subjects based in the UK or the services provided involve the monitoring of their behaviour.

136. There are fifteen standards set out in the Children's code. The standards do not create new law as such. The overarching goal of the standards is to identify how data controllers and data processors can fulfil their obligations to children, when personal data is processed during the course of accessing information society services and use of digital technologies. In addition to operationalising the aspirations set out in the recitals which make references to safeguarding children and promoting their rights, the code places the onus on information society services providers to demonstrate to uphold the standards and demonstrate compliance with these.[268] The code can be taken into account as evidence of inactions for non-compliance with data protection legislation or the Privacy and Electronic Communications (EC Directive) Regulations 2003.[269] The fifteen standards are:

(1) Best interests of the child.
(2) DPIAs
(3) Age-appropriate application
(4) Transparency
(5) Detrimental use of data
(6) Policies and community standards
(7) Default settings
(8) Data minimisation
(9) Data sharing
(10) Geolocation
(11) Parental controls
(12) Profiling

266. Section 123(4) and (7). The Commissioner is also required to have regard to the UK's obligations as a signatory to the United Nations Convention on the Rights of the Child.
267. Section 123(1) of the DPA 2018.
268. *See* Recitals 7 and 38. *See also* the Information Commissioner's references to the promotion of children's rights and safeguarding – available on website.
269. Section 127 of the DPA 2018.

(13) Nudge techniques
(14) Connected toys and devices
(15) Online tools.

137. A brief observation can be made with regard to some of the standard setting features in the age-appropriate code. The extension of the best interests of the child principle to include private sector entities such as information services providers should be seen not as creating a set of legally enforceable obligations such as those the UK GDPR creates in favour of data subjects against data controllers and data processors. The best interests of the child standard can be seen as aspirational, keeping in mind the overarching ethical imperative as set out in Recital 38:

> Children merit specific protection with regard to their personal data, as they may be less aware of the risks, consequences and safeguards concerned and their rights in relation to the processing of personal data. Such specific protection should, in particular, apply to the use of personal data of children for the purposes of marketing or creating personality or user profiles and the collection of personal data with regard to children when using services offered directly to a child.

138. Personal data of children will now be included in the list of the type of processing operations where a DPIA is mandatory.[270] Processing of children's personal data is now regarded as 'high-risk' and data controllers will require to undertake an assessment of whether the 'nature, scope, context and purposes of the processing, is likely to result in a high risk to the rights and freedoms' of the child. Other standards such as age-appropriate application, transparency, detrimental use of data, policies and community standards, default settings, data minimisation, data sharing and geolocation aim to ensure that appropriate safeguards for children so that risks resulting from the processing of their personal data do not arise or minimised. The Commissioner has provided additional resources to guide decision-making. Annex B provides information for information services providers about the developmental stages of children and the considerations that need to be borne in mind when dealing with pre-literate (0–5 years), core primary (6–9 years), transition (10–12 years), early teen (13–15 years) and approaching adulthood (16–17 years). Annex C provides guidance on the lawful basis for processing with particular focus on using default settings as norm to ensure that there is a compelling reason for departure. Devices used by children will have geolocation data switched off as default, to ensure that the child is not subjected to covert monitoring or commercial surveillance. The profiling standard draws on the UK GDPR, emphasising the need to respect the dignity of children as persons and individuals by extending protection to the use of 'personal data of children for the purposes of marketing or creating personality or user profiles and the collection of personal data with regard to children when using services offered directly to a child.'[271]

---

270. Article 35(4) of the UK GDPR.
271. Recital 38 UK GDPR. *See also* Recital 71 UK GDPR.

139. The data sharing code came into force on 5 October 2021. The data sharing code was developed under section 121 of the DPA 2018. The standards governing data sharing aim to set out a number of requirements which organisations are expected to comply with. Additionally the data sharing code also provides guidance that the Commissioner considers 'appropriate to promote good practice in the sharing of personal data'.[272] Sharing for the purposes of the code is deemed to take place as soon as there is a 'disclosure of personal data by transmission, dissemination or otherwise making it available'.[273] Consequently, transmission or disclosure will cover sharing not only of personal data in the public sector but also between and by entities in the private sector. The sharing of personal data is not restricted to the use of particular means. Providing a third party with access to the organisation's dataset via its IT system, exchanging personal data as well as receiving personal data as part of a data sharing agreement would be covered by the code. Routine sharing of personal data between organisations for established purpose or purposes or agreements to pool or share personal data would be covered by the code. The code provides checklists (Annex A) which help organisations consider particular factors when making decisions about entering into data sharing agreements (Annex A) or responding to requests for access to personal data (Annex B). Annex C provides case studies that provide organisations with an opportunity to reflect on the necessity for data sharing, assessment of risks, the processes for ensuring transparency and accountability and steps to be taken to promote public trust in the way personal data is being handled. More generally, the code provides important guidance particularly where the personal data to be shared concerns children, response to a one-off situation or in an emergency, the conduct of a DPIA, the lawful and fair grounds for processing and more broadly the sharing of data across the public sector. Data sharing within the same organisation is not covered by the code. This is understandable as the processing of personal data is already subjected to extensive obligations under data protection law. Furthermore, providing access to personal data to an employee or third-party IT processors would not be regarded as a form of data sharing.[274]

140. Given that anonymised data is not regarded as personal data, the data sharing code does not prohibit such forms of disclosure or transmission. However, if there is every likelihood that the individual can be easily identified by combining different datasets or combining the data with other information, the disclosure would be regarded as data sharing. Disclosure of pseudonymised data will be treated as sharing as additional information can be used to identify the individual. The failure of a person or organisation to act in accordance with the code does not of itself create a presumption of non-compliance in respect of liability should there be legal proceedings in a court or tribunal.[275] However, the code can be introduced in legal

272. Section 121(1) (b) of the DPA 2018.
273. Section 121(5) of the DPA 2018.
274. Reference should be made to the Commissioner's guidance on anonymisation.
275. Section 127(1) of the DPA 2018.

proceedings as admissible evidence. The legal proceedings concerned need not necessarily be confined to issues about violation of data protection obligations.[276]

141. The data sharing code can be seen as a much-needed policy development given the exponential growth in the collection, processing and sharing of personal data taking place not only in the private sector but also in the public sector. The code does not create new law. Its primary role is to provide guidance to organisations on how to comply with best practice on sharing data fairly and lawfully in a transparent and accountable manner. One intended outcome of the data sharing code is that it aims to address any 'misconceptions about data sharing and barriers to sharing'.[277] As noted previously, the code on data sharing does not have legal status, but the ICO must take the provisions in the code into account when considering whether an organisation has complied with its data protection obligations when sharing data. The code is also admissible as evidence in court or tribunal proceedings, where it is relevant to the issue being considered.

142. There are a number of notable features in the code on data sharing. The code governs the sharing of personal data between controllers. Given the risks that may arise from the sharing of personal data, controllers are advised to carry out a DPIA with a view to identifying any risks as well as measures to mitigate the adverse effects. As part of the transparency and accountability process, data sharing agreements are recommended. The aim here is to delineate the purpose of the data sharing activity, the use made by data at each state, standards, and the respective roles and responsibilities of parties in the data sharing agreement. The ICO has developed model data sharing agreement forms, which include provisions for consent (where that is the legal basis for processing), and forms for requesting and approving sharing of data. Particular prominence is given to sharing children's personal data. The code emphasises the heightened risks involved with sharing children's personal and recommends that sharing should not take place unless it can be demonstrated that there is a compelling reason to do so, taking account of the best interests of the child principle. In cases where personal data of children is to be shared, a DPIA is recommended together with due diligence checks on the recipient organisation. The aim of the precautionary risk-based approach is to ensure that risks are clearly identified and assessed so that the rights and freedoms of children, which arise from the data sharing, are not compromised. The code has provisions governing the parties responsible for compliance with the UK GDPR and DPA 2018, the adoption of a 'data protection by design and default' approach, audits and appropriate documentation (e.g., Article 30 records, Data Sharing Agreements, DPIAs) and complementary reporting and monitoring measures. Many of the provisions in the code aim to map the responsibility of controllers under Article 5 of the UK GDPR and the fairness, security and transparency provisions in the UK GDPR more generally. For example, under the code, controllers are encouraged to

276. *See* s. 127(2) of the DPA 2018. *See also* the function of the Commissioner under s. 127(4).
277. *See* ICO Data Sharing Code https://ico.org.uk/for-organisations/guide-to-data-protection/ico-codes-of-practice/data-sharing-a-code-of-practice/about-this-code/.

treat individuals fairly and not in ways that overreach the data minimisation and purpose limitation principles. The code also makes clear that the mere fact that data can be shared should not absolve controllers and recipients to consider their ethical obligations – namely 'whether it is right to share'. The code stresses the importance and value of integrating into data sharing agreements, policies and processes that enable data subjects to exercise their rights and that information is provided to this end in a way that is clear and accessible. In cases where the data sharing arrangement involves solely automated processing, extra measures to safeguard the rights of data subjects (as set out in both the DPA 2018 and UK GDPR) are recommended. The code also makes provision for data sharing arising from a merger or acquisition as well as sharing of personal data in databases and lists.

§2. Codes under the UK GDPR

143. Under Article 40(1) of the UK GDPR, the Information Commissioner can encourage the drawing up of codes of conduct intended to contribute to the proper application of this Regulation, taking account of the specific features of the various processing sectors and the specific needs of micro, small and medium-sized enterprises.[278] An ICO-approved UK GDPR code is commonly prepared by a body able to legitimately speak on behalf of a group of organisations, such as a trade or representative body. The code should provide a detailed description of what the UK GDPR means in practice for the organisations it covers, focusing on key data protection priorities and challenges that they are facing. Such codes should aim to outline technical and organisational measures that controllers and processors must have in place in order to be a member of the code of conduct. A key feature of ICO-approved UK GDPR codes is the in-built mechanism for monitoring an organisations' compliance with the code.

§3. Codes under the UK GDPR: Nature and Scope

144. The national supervisory authority, the Information Commissioner can encourage associations and representatives of controllers or processors in the private and public sectors to draw up codes to ensure that data protection rules are applied consistently (Recital 98). Codes are developed to 'contribute to the proper application of this Regulation' (Article 40(1)). Organisations interested in developing codes are encouraged to engage in informal discussions as a step before making a formal submission. The guidance (available on the website) includes the steps to

278. Words in Art. 40(1) substituted (31.12.2020) by The Data Protection, Privacy and Electronic Communications (Amendments etc.) (EU Exit) Regulations 2019 (S.I. 2019/419), reg. 1(2), Sch. 1 para. 34(2) (with reg. 5); 2020 c. 1, Sch. 5 para. 1(1).

be taken when developing codes, the timelines and processes for submission, and a checklist for assessing compliance with submission criteria and the approval process.[279]

145. Codes serve as useful instruments for standard setting in organisations that are not confined to applying data protection rules and can be seen as setting a benchmark for compliance. As noted above, codes can be used to ensure that the processing activities complement the legal standards and meet the specific requirements of various sectors and contexts. Organisations engaged with the processing of personal data can develop codes which ensure the consistent application of data protection rules, that processing is transparent and fair and that the purposes for which processing is undertaken are clearly understood by data subjects. From a risk management perspective, codes can provide a framework which streamlines the processes for impact assessment, monitoring and notification of non-compliance or breaches. Data controllers can rely on codes to demonstrate their compliance with their accountability obligations.[280] To ensure that the codes are useful mechanisms for standard setting, Article 40(1) of the UK GDPR requires that 'account of the specific features of the various processing sectors and the specific needs of micro, small and medium-sized enterprises' must be taken into account. Furthermore, Recital 98 provides that associations or bodies representing data controllers or data processors:

> should be encouraged to draw up codes of conduct, within the limits of this Regulation, so as to facilitate the effective application of this Regulation, taking account of the specific characteristics of the processing carried out in certain sectors and the specific needs of micro, small and medium enterprises. In particular, such codes of conduct could calibrate the obligations of controllers and processors, taking into account the risk likely to result from the processing for the rights and freedoms of natural persons.

§4. Codes under the UK GDPR: Competence and Scope

146. As a general rule associations or bodies representing categories of controllers or processors can assume the responsibility for preparing codes. Codes can cover a wide range of processing operations and activities involving data controllers or processors:[281]

- fair and transparent processing;
- the legitimate interests pursued by controllers in specific contexts;
- the collection of personal data;
- the pseudonymisation of personal data;

279. The updated documents are available on the ICO website: https://ico.org.uk/for-organisations/guide-to-data-protection/guide-to-the-general-data-protection-regulation-gdpr/codes-of-conduct-detailed-guidance/how-do-we-gain-monitoring-body-accreditation/#12.
280. *See* UK GDPR Arts 24, 28 and 32. Cf. Art. 41(4).
281. Article 40(2).

- the information provided to the public and to data subjects;
- the exercise of the rights of data subjects;
- the information provided to, and the protection of, children, and the manner in which the consent of the holders of parental responsibility over children is to be obtained;
- the measures and procedures referred to in Articles 24 and 25 and the measures to ensure security of processing referred to in Article 32;
- the notification of personal data breaches to the Commissioner and the communication of such personal data breaches to data subjects;
- the transfer of personal data to third countries or international organisations; or
- out-of-court proceedings and other dispute resolution procedures for resolving disputes between controllers and data subjects with regard to processing, without prejudice to the rights of data subjects pursuant to Articles 77 and 79.

147. However, by virtue of Article 40(4) of the UK GDPR codes that involve particular categories of processing of personal data as set out in Article 40(2), will require prior approval and must contain mechanisms for monitoring by an independent authority.[282]

§5. Codes under the UK GDPR: Monitoring and Accreditation of Monitoring Bodies

148. Monitoring of compliance with codes may be undertaken by bodies which have the 'appropriate level of expertise in relation to the subject-matter of the code' and has been accredited for that purpose by the Information Commissioner. For a body to be accredited, it needs to demonstrate its independence and expertise of the code that meets the expectations of the competent supervisory authority.[283] The threshold for meeting the expectations includes demonstrating that the undertaking of the tasks and duties does not give rise to conflict of interest, has established internal procedures and mechanisms for assessing the eligibility of controllers and processors concerned, monitoring compliance, periodical review of its operation and transparent processes for managing complaints about violations of codes, and accessible to the data subject and public. Under Article 57(1)(p) of the UK GDPR, the Information Commissioner has the responsibility to draft and publish the requirements for accreditation of a body for monitoring codes of conduct pursuant to Article 41 and of a certification body pursuant to Article 43.[284] Accreditation is not permanent. It is subject to a process of review, and particular instances, can be revoked. Accreditation can be revoked if it is shown that the requirements for accreditation are not, or are no longer, met or where actions taken by the body were

---

282. *See also* Art. 41(4) and 41(1).
283. Article 41(2).
284. *See also* Art. 41(3). Note that post-withdrawal from the EU, Opinions of the European Data Protection Board are not binding on the ICO. That said *see* EDPB Guidelines 1/2019 on Codes of Conduct and Monitoring Bodies.

found to have infringed the Regulation.[285] Revocation may be temporary or permanent. The type of circumstances that will lead to a permanent withdrawal of accreditation would include a failure to discharge key monitoring body requirements such as ensuring no conflict of interests, lack of expertise or independence, failing to monitor compliance by code members, or persistent complaints made by code members about the monitoring body's discharge of its responsibilities.

§6. Codes under the UK GDPR: Certification

149. Recital 100 regards 'certification mechanisms and data protection seals and marks' as instruments for enhancing transparency and compliance obligations assumed under data protection law. Article 42(1) alludes to the use of indicators or signifiers that the product or service meets appropriate standards and/or compliance by the controllers and processors with data protection obligations. The UK GDPR makes a number of references to certification. For example, Article 25(3) states that an approved certification mechanism pursuant to Article 42 may be used as an element to demonstrate compliance with the obligations under the data protection by design and default provision. Certification can also be a way to demonstrate that the data controller has put in place appropriate technical and organisational measures to ensure a level of security appropriate to the risk, with regard to:[286]

- the pseudonymisation and encryption of personal data;
- the ability to ensure the ongoing confidentiality, integrity, availability and resilience of processing systems and services;
- the ability to restore the availability and access to personal data in a timely manner in the event of a physical or technical incident;
- a process for regularly testing, assessing and evaluating the effectiveness of technical and organisational measures for ensuring the security of the processing.

150. Certification is a voluntary process.[287] Controllers or processors may wish to demonstrate compliance with data protection obligations and standards by including certification in their contractual relationship.[288] The mere fact that the processing operation is underpinned by certification, does not absolve the controller or the processor for compliance with the specific transparency and accountability provisions in data protection law.[289]

151. As noted previously, certification can be provided by certification bodies in pursuance of Article 43 by the Commissioner. The controller or processor whose processing operation is governed by the certification mechanism must provide the

285. Article 41(5).
286. Article 32(3) and 32(1).
287. Article 42(3).
288. Article 42(2).
289. Article 42(4).

certification body with all relevant information and access to its processing activities.[290] Certification is only available for a period no longer than three years. It may be renewed on the grounds that the relevant criteria continue to be met. Certification can however be withdrawn at any time by the certification body or by the Commissioner where the conditions for certification are not being met. The Commissioner has the responsibility for collating all certification mechanisms and data protection seals and marks in a register.[291] These are publicly accessible on the ICO website.[292]

§7. Direct Marketing Code of Practice

152. The Information Commissioner has updated its direct marketing code of practice following the measures introduced by the UK GDPR. Section 122(1) of the DPA 2018 requires the Commissioner to prepare a code of practice. The Commissioner prepared a draft code which provides 'practical guidance in relation to the carrying out of direct marketing' and any other guidance considered appropriate to promote good practice in accordance with the obligations under data protection legislation and the Privacy and Electronic Communications Regulations (EC Directive) Regulations. 'Direct marketing' covers communications by whatever means of advertising or marketing material which is directed to particular individuals.[293] The DPA 2018 sets out a procedure for approval of the code as is the case with other statutory codes. The Commissioner is required to consult the Secretary of State as well as trade associations, data subjects and bodies or entities representing the interests of data subjects.[294] In addition to this, the Commissioner is required to submit the final version to the Secretary of State, and the code must be laid before both Houses of Parliament.[295] Under the negative period, set out in section 125(3) of the DPA 2018, if either House of Parliament resolves not to approve the code within the forty-day period, the code must not be issued. If no resolution has been made within that period, the Commissioner must issue the code, and it comes into force at the end of the period of twenty-one days beginning with the day on which it is issued.[296] A draft code was issued for public consultation, which closed in March 2020, shortly before the pandemic. Work on the code was paused, and a final version is currently being prepared and will be made available on the ICO website when completed.

290. Article 42(5) and (6).
291. Article 42(8).
292. Article 42(5). *See* https://ico.org.uk/for-organisations/certification-schemes-register/.
293. Section 122(5) of the DPA 2018.
294. Section 122(3).
295. Section 125(1) of the DPA 2018.
296. Section 125(4).

Part VII. International Transfers

Chapter 1. General Principles

153. It should be recalled that on 28 June 2021, the Commission adopted two adequacy decisions (one pursuant to the GDPR and the other pursuant to the LED)[297] confirming that the UK ensures a level of protection for personal data transferred from the EU that is 'essentially equivalent' to the one guaranteed by EU data protection law.[298] The Commission retains the power to suspend or terminate the adequacy findings and its assessment is time-limited: both adequacy decisions contain a 'sunset clause', which limits the duration of adequacy to four years.[299]

154. The legal framework on international transfers of personal data from the United Kingdom to third countries is laid down in Articles 44, 45, 46, 47 and 49 of the UK GDPR,[300] which replicate without any material changes the relevant rules of the GDPR. Essentially, under the UK GDPR, transfers of personal data to a third country or international organisation can only take place on the basis of adequacy regulations,[301] or in the absence of those, on the basis of appropriate safeguards in accordance with Article 46 of the UK GDPR. In the absence of adequacy regulations or appropriate safeguards, a transfer can only take place based on the derogations provided in Article 49 of the UK GDPR.

155. Adequacy regulations providing that a third country or an international organisation ensures an adequate level of protection of personal data are adopted by the Secretary of State. When assessing the adequacy of the level of protection, the Secretary of State must take into account the elements included in Article 45(2)(a)–(c) GDPR.[302] Before adopting adequacy regulations, the Secretary of State

297. European Commission, Commission Implementing Decision of 28.6.2021 pursuant to Regulation (EU) 2016/679 of the European Parliament and of the Council on the adequate protection of personal data by the United Kingdom, C(2021) 4800 final and Commission Implementing Decision of 28.6.2021 pursuant to Directive (EU) 2016/680 of the European Parliament and of the Council on the adequate protection of personal data by the United Kingdom, C(2021) 4801 final. *See also* Maria Tzanou and Spyridoula Karyda, 'Privacy International and Quadrature du Net: One Step Forward Two Steps Back in the Data Retention Saga?' *European Public Law* 28 (1), (2022) pp. 123–154, 148–149.
298. *Ibid.*, Art. 1.
299. Both decisions will expire on 27 Jun. 2025.
300. Article 48 GDPR has not been included in the UK GDPR.
301. These are equivalent to 'adequacy decisions'.
302. The elements are the same as the ones used by the Commission to assess adequacy.

must consult the ICO.[303] Adequacy regulations are subject to the 'negative resolution procedure'.[304] This means that once adopted by the Secretary of State, those regulations are subject to annulment under a resolution of either House of Parliament.

156. In the absence of an adequacy regulation, personal data may be transferred to a third country or an international organisation only if the controller or processor has provided appropriate safeguards in accordance with Article 46 of the UK GDPR. These safeguards, which correspond to the ones enshrined in Article 46 of the GDPR, include legally binding and enforceable instruments between public authorities or bodies, BCRs,[305] standard data protection clauses adopted by the Secretary of State or the ICO, approved codes of conduct and approved certification mechanisms. International data transfers can also take place by using contractual clauses authorised by the ICO.

157. In the absence of an adequacy regulation or appropriate safeguards, a transfer can only take place based on derogations set out in Article 49 of the UK GDPR, which contains the same set of reasons as the GDPR. The Secretary of State may by regulations specify, for the purposes of Article 49(1)(d) of the UK GDPR circumstances in which a transfer of personal data to a third country or international organisation is to be taken to be necessary for important reasons of public interest.[306] The Secretary of State may by regulations also restrict the transfer of a category of personal data to a third country or international organisation where the Secretary of State considers the restriction to be necessary for important reasons of public interest.[307]

303. Section 182 of the DPA 2018. *See also* the Memorandum of Understanding (MoU) on the role of the ICO in relation to new UK adequacy assessments https://www.gov.uk/government/publications/memorandum-of-understanding-mou-on-the-role-of-the-ico-in-relation-to-new-uk-adequacy-assessments.
304. Section 182(6) of the DPA 2018.
305. *See* Art. 47 of the UK GDPR.
306. Section 18(1) of the DPA 2018.
307. Section 18(2) of the DPA 2018.

Chapter 2. Transfers in the Context of International Agreements (e.g., Mutual Legal Assistance Treaties)

158. Further to the legal framework discussed above regarding international data transfers, the United Kingdom regime on international transfers for law enforcement purposes (including mutual legal assistance treaties (MLATs)) is regulated by Chapter 5 of Part 3 of the DPA 2018. Part 3 of the DPA 2018 aims to implement the LED in UK law and constitutes the so-called EU-derived domestic legislation.[308] In order to transfer personal data to a third country, a competent authority must meet the following conditions: (a) the transfer must be necessary for a law enforcement purpose; (b) the transfer must be based on: (i) an adequacy regulation in respect of the third country, (ii) if not based on an adequacy regulation, appropriate safeguards must exist, or (iii) if not based on an adequacy decision or appropriate safeguards, it must be based on special circumstances.[309]

159. In *Elgizouli v. Secretary of State for the Home Department*,[310] the UK Supreme Court had to consider whether the Home Secretary's decision to transfer evidence to the United States (US) under the UK-US MLAT 1994 was lawful. The evidence, which was obtained by British authorities, concerned two individuals suspected of committing crimes in Syria, including the murder of twenty-seven people in recorded beheadings, which were subsequently posted online. The case was brought by one of the individuals' father, who argued that the information transferred to the US authorities could facilitate their persecution for offences that might result in the imposition of the death penalty. The Supreme Court had to adjudicate on two points: (i) whether it was unlawful at common law for the Government to facilitate the carrying out of the death penalty in a foreign state, not only by deporting or removing a person from the United Kingdom to be tried in that state but also by providing information which may be used by that state in the trial of a person who is not currently in the United Kingdom; (ii) whether the decision to provide such information, insofar as it consisted of personal data within the meaning of the DPA 2018, was unlawful under Part 3 of that Act.[311] The Supreme Court rejected the first claim at common law but found that the transfer was unlawful because it breached the DPA 2018.[312] It held that:

> Insofar as the information provided, or to be provided, to the US authorities consisted of personal data (which much of it did) the processing of such data by the Secretary of State as data controller required a conscious, contemporaneous consideration of whether the criteria for such processing were met. 'Substantial compliance' with those criteria, as found by the Divisional Court, is not

308. *See* below.
309. Section 75(1)(a) of the DPA 2018.
310. [2020] UKSC 10.
311. *Ibid.*, para. 3.
312. *Ibid.*, para. 6.

enough. It is not in dispute that the Secretary of State, when making the decision in question, did not address his mind to the 2018 Act at all.[313]

160. Lady Hale then cited Recitals 1, 17 and 46 of the LED – which Part 3 of the DPA 2018 implements – concluding that the fundamental rights and freedoms of the data subject referred to in section 76(2) of the DPA 2018 'must include the rights protected by the European Convention. These are to apply even where the data are to be transferred to a third country outside the European Union and whatever the nationality or place of residence of the data subject'.[314] According to the Supreme Court, collectively, the Part 3 of the DPA 2018 provisions point towards an interpretation of section 76(2) 'which would not allow the transfer of personal data to facilitate a prosecution which could result in the death penalty; but which would allow such a transfer if it was urgently necessary to save life or prevent an imminent crime'.[315]

161. The judgment is particularly important given the various forms of specific cooperation for the onward transfer of personal data from the UK to third countries, and in particular, the USA.[316] For instance, in 2019 the UK concluded an agreement with the US 'on Access to Electronic Data for the Purpose of Countering Serious Crime'.[317] The UK-US Agreement was adopted under the US Clarifying Lawful Overseas Use of Data (CLOUD) Act, which requires that US communication service providers are obliged to comply with US orders to disclose content and non-content data, regardless of where such data is stored.[318] Unlike traditional cross-border law enforcement mechanisms, such as MLATs, under which requests for data might take significant time, the UK-US Agreement purports to avoid these time-consuming inter-State mechanisms by allowing national authorities to request data directly from service providers, subject to a number of conditions and safeguards.[319] The Agreement raises several data protection issues and may impact the level of protection assessed in the adequacy decision regarding the UK.[320] For this reason, the European Commission has clearly stated in the adequacy decision that the UK must ensure proper monitoring of its obligations in line with Article 45 (4)

313. *Ibid.*
314. *Ibid.*, para. 13.
315. *Ibid.*, para. 15.
316. This issue was raised in the Commission's decision on the adequate protection of personal data by the United Kingdom, because 'data transferred from the EU to service providers in the United Kingdom could be subject to orders for the production of electronic evidence issued by competent US law enforcement authorities'. *See* adequacy decision, *supra* 154, Recitals 153–155.
317. UK/USA: Agreement on Access to Electronic Data for the Purpose of Countering Serious Crime [CS USA No.6/2019] https://www.gov.uk/government/publications/ukusa-agreement-on-access-to-electronic-data-for-the-purpose-of-countering-serious-crime-cs-usa-no62019. The Agreement entered into force on 8 July 2020.
318. US Cloud Act https://www.congress.gov/115/bills/s2383/BILLS-115s2383is.pdf.
319. *See* Theodore Christakis, '21 Thoughts and Questions about the UK/US CLOUD Act Agreement (and an Explanation of How it Works – with Charts)', (13 October 2019). European Law Blog, Available at SSRN: https://ssrn.com/abstract=3469704 and Eddie B. Kim, 'U.S.-UK Executive Agreement: Case Study of Incidental Collection of Data under the CLOUD Act' (2020) 15 *Wash J L Tech & Arts* 247.
320. *See* adequacy decision, *supra* 154, Recital 155.

of the GDPR and particular attention must be given to the application and adaptation of the Umbrella Agreement's protections to the specific type of transfers covered by the UK-US Agreement.[321] The Commission has also confirmed that it will duly take into account 'any relevant development as regards the entry into force and application of the Agreement' in the context of its continuous monitoring of the UK adequacy decision, 'including with respect to the necessary consequences to be drawn in case of any indication that an essentially equivalent level of protection is no longer ensured'.[322]

---

321. *Ibid.*
322. *Ibid.*, Recital 156.

Part VIII. Enforcement

Chapter 1. Supervisory Authorities

162. The DPA 2018 provides that the Office of the Information Commissioner is the relevant supervisory authority for the purposes of the UK GDPR and the DPA 2018.[323] The Commissioner oversees the enforcement of the UK GDPR, and Pts 3 and 4 of the DPA 2018 that cover personal data processing for law enforcement and intelligence purposes, respectively.[324] The Information Commissioner is also the designated authority in the UK under Article 13 of Convention 108+.[325] This means that the ICO is 'the supervisory authority for all the data protection regimes'[326] in the UK.

163. Under the previous regime of the DPA 1998, the ICO's activities were funded by fee income raised by the notification process, which has now been abolished.[327] Indeed, Article 57(3) of the EU GDPR requires that the performance of the tasks of supervisory authorities should be 'free of charge for the data subject and, where applicable, for the data protection officer'. The DPA 2018 allows the ICO to charge fees in three instances: 'reasonable' fees to be paid for services provided to a person other than a data subject or a DPO;[328] fees in respect of manifestly unfounded or excessive requests from a data subject or a DPO;[329] and, charges payable to the Commissioner by controllers set by the Secretary of State regulations.[330]

323. Section 114(1) of the DPA 2018.
324. Schedule 13 para. 1(1) of DPA 2018.
325. Section 116(2) of the DPA 2018.
326. Jay, *supra*, 967.
327. Jay, *supra*, 975.
328. Section 134 of the DPA 2018.
329. Section 135 of the DPA 2018.
330. Section 137 of the DPA 2018. *See also* Data Protection Charges and Information Regulations 2018. The ICO is also funded by 'grant in aid' that is used to finance its operating costs regarding non-data protection related tasks.

Chapter 2. Composition

164. The Information Commissioner is regarded as a 'corporation sole':[331] a legal entity constituted in a single person office-holder.[332] This form of corporate personality 'allows for continuity of legal responsibility where the office holder changes'.[333] Currently, the UK Information Commissioner is John Edwards. The Information Commissioner is supported in their work by an office. The Commissioner may employ the staff they deem appropriate.[334] The Commissioner and their staff are not considered Crown servants.[335] As of 31 March 2021, the ICO had 822 permanent staff.[336]

165. Article 52 of the UK GDPR, which retains without any material changes the relevant provision of the GDPR, establishes the independence of the Commissioner. The Commissioner is an independent official answerable directly to the Parliament and not to the Government. The Information Commissioner is an executive non-departmental public body and exercises the legal powers vested to them as a corporation sole.[337] The sponsoring department for the ICO within the Government is the Department for Digital, Culture Media and Sport (DCMS).[338]

166. Schedule 12 to the DPA 2018 provides the conditions for the appointment and removal of the Information Commissioner. The Information Commissioner is appointed by Her Majesty by Letters Patent on a recommendation from Government. The person concerned must be selected on merit on the basis of fair and open competition. The Commissioner may hold office for a period not exceeding seven years. A person cannot be appointed as Commissioner more than once.

167. The Information Commissioner can be relieved of office by the Queen at their own request, but they can only be removed from office by the Queen following an address by both Houses of Parliament.[339] No such motion for dismissal can be made to either House of Parliament unless a Minister has presented a report to that House stating that they are satisfied that the Commissioner is guilty of serious misconduct and/ or the Commissioner no longer fulfils the conditions required for the performance of the Commissioner's functions.[340]

---

331. Schedule 12(1) DPA 2018.
332. *See* adequacy decision, *supra* 154, Recital 86.
333. Jay, *supra*, 973.
334. *Ibid.*, 975.
335. Schedule 12(2) DPA 2018.
336. ICO, Information Commissioner's Annual Report and Financial Statements 2020-21 https://ico.org.uk/media/about-the-ico/documents/2620166/hc-354-information-commissioners-ara-2020-21.pdf.
337. Jay, *supra*, 973.
338. *See* Management agreement 2018–2021 which has been extended to 2022 https://ico.org.uk/media/about-the-ico/documents/2259800/management-agreement-2018-2021.pdf.
339. Schedule 12(3) DPA 2018.
340. Schedule 12(3)(3) DPA 2018.

Chapter 3. Competence, Tasks and Powers

168. The general tasks and powers of the Information Commissioner are set out in Articles 57 and 58 of the UK GDPR which closely reflects the corresponding rules of the EU GDPR. More particularly, the Commissioner's tasks include, among others, monitoring and enforcement of the UK GDPR, investigative tasks, promoting public awareness, dealing with complaints lodged by the data subjects, issuing data protection audits. The Commissioner's functions also include a duty to advise Parliament, the government and other institutions and bodies on legislative and administrative measures relating to the protection of individuals' rights and freedoms with regard to the processing of personal data, and a power to issue, on the Commissioner's own initiative or on request, opinions to Parliament, the government or other institutions and bodies as well as to the public on any issue related to the protection of personal data.[341]

169. The Commissioner has extensive investigatory and enforcement powers. They may, by a written notice (an 'information notice'), require a controller or processor to provide information that the Commissioner reasonably requires for the purposes of carrying out their functions under the data protection legislation.[342] The ICO may by written notice (an 'assessment notice') require a controller or processor to permit the Commissioner to carry out an assessment of whether the controller or processor has complied or is complying with the data protection legislation. An assessment notice may require the controller or processor to permit the Commissioner to enter specified premises; direct the Commissioner to equipment or other material on the premises which is of a specified description; permit the Commissioner to inspect or examine the documents, information, equipment or material to which the Commissioner is directed or which the Commissioner is assisted to view; permit the Commissioner to observe the processing of personal data that takes place on the premises; and, make available for interview people who process personal data on behalf of the controller.[343] Furthermore, the Commissioner has powers of entry and inspection[344] and can issue 'enforcement notices' if a person is failing to comply with the provisions of the UK GDPR or the DPA 2018.[345] Finally, the ICO can issue 'penalty notices'.[346]

341. Section 115(3) of the DPA 2018.
342. Section 142 of the DPA 2018.
343. Section 146 of the DPA 2018.
344. Section 154 of the DPA 2018.
345. Section 149 of the DPA 2018.
346. Section 155 of the DPA 2018.

Chapter 4. Remedies

170. Data protection law provides data subjects with a number of rights such as the right to object, right to access and rights to portability. In addition to these rights a data subject also has other mechanisms or avenues for enforcement: complaints to the Commissioner, judicial remedies for compensation or recourse to representative actions.[347]

§1. Complaints to the Information Commissioner

171. Section 165 of the DPA 2018 sets out a framework through which complaints regarding violations of data protection rights can be made to the Information Commissioner.[348] It is worth noting that this mechanism for resolving grievances mirrors those made available under the EU GDPR. For example, Article 77 provides that a data subject can lodge a complaint with the Commissioner for breaches of the UK GDPR.[349] A data subject relying on this mechanism must establish that the complaint is in respect of those rights which he or she regard as being infringed by the processing of personal data that relates to him or her.[350] The use of this complaint procedure is made without prejudice to the data subject's right to any other administrative or judicial remedy.[351] The Information Commissioner is under an obligation to keep the data subject informed on the progress and the outcome of the complaint, including the possibility of a judicial remedy pursuant to Article 78.[352]

172. As to the administrative and procedural steps to be taken when processing complaints, we can elicit some general ideas about what these may involve by turning the framework provided for addressing violations of data subject's rights under section 165 of the DPA 2018.[353] The Information Commissioner is, for example, required to facilitate the making of complaints.[354] This includes taking administrative steps such as providing the data subject with a complaint form. The form can be completed electronically and by other means. Section 165(3) of the DPA 2018 requires the Commissioner, on receipt of the complaint, to take appropriate steps to

347. Part 3 of the Data Protection Act 2018 contains a number of provisions which implement the Law Enforcement Directive. Part 4 of the Data Protection Act 2018 sets out provisions for breaches of data subjects rights by intelligence services.
348. Words in s. 165(1) substituted (31.12.2020) by The Data Protection, Privacy and Electronic Communications (Amendments etc) (EU Exit) Regulations 2019 (S.I. 2019/419), reg. 1(2), Sch. 2 para. 66(2) (with reg. 5); 2020 c. 1, Sch. 5 para. 1(1).
349. Words in Art. 77 heading substituted (31.12.2020) by The Data Protection, Privacy and Electronic Communications (Amendments etc) (EU Exit) Regulations 2019 (S.I. 2019/419), reg. 1(2), Sch. 1 para. 56(2) (with reg. 5); 2020 c. 1, Sch. 5 para. 1(1).
350. Article 77(1) of the UK GDPR and s. 165(1) of the DPA 2018. Section 165(2) of the DPA 2018 relates to processing of personal data under Parts 3 and 4 of the legislation.
351. Article 78(1) and (2) of the UK GDPR. Also Art. 79 of the UK GDPR with regard to an effective judicial remedy against a controller or processor.
352. Article 77(2) of the UK GDPR.
353. Section 165(2) of the DPA 2018.
354. Section 165(3).

inform the complainant of the progress and outcome together with recourse to rights under section 166 of the DPA 2018. This section allows the complainant to apply to the Tribunal if the Information Commissioner has not progressed the complaint appropriately. If requested, the Information Commissioner must provide further information to the individual on how to pursue the complaint. This last mechanism can be seen as an example of providing an effective judicial remedy where the supervisory authority is alleged to have not handled the complaint properly,[355] and it is one that is also found in Article 78(2) of the UK GDPR. The powers of the Tribunal, which are set out in section 166(2) of the DPA 2018, permit it to make an order requiring the Information Commissioner either to take appropriate steps to respond to the complaint, or to inform the complainant of progress on the complaint, or of the outcome of the complaint, within a period specified in the order. The order may consist of requiring the Information Commissioner to take steps specified in the order or to conclude an investigation, or take a specified step, within a period specified in the order. The limits to the power of the Tribunal are sometimes overlooked. In *Bright Jemwa*, the applicant seemed to view the section 166 of the DPA 2018 mechanism as a right of appeal against the substantive outcome of the Commissioner's ruling.[356] The application for an order to progress a complaint under section 166 of the DPA 2018 was dismissed. The Tribunal observed that it did not have the powers of reviewing investigations on their merits and viewed the application as tantamount to an order requiring rectification of the complainant's personal data, which it held was not within its competence.[357] The Tribunal also observed in passing that appropriate steps had been taken by the Information Commissioner to communicate the outcome of the complaint to the applicant. Section 166 of the DPA 2018 mechanism is best viewed as a mechanism for ensuring the procedural fairness of the complaints handling process, namely to assess whether the Information Commissioner had failed to take appropriate steps when responding to a complaint, or failed to update the data subject on progress or the outcome of the complaint.[358] The key point about the procedural fairness aspect is that 'appropriate steps' be taken to respond to the complaint rather than taking steps to produce an appropriate outcome that meets with the approval of the applicant.[359]

§2. Judicial Remedies

173. Article 79(1) of the UK GDPR provides that data subjects have the right to an effective judicial remedy against data controllers and processors. The right to an effective judicial remedy is restricted to those rights deemed to have been infringed as a result of the processing of his or her personal data in non-compliance with this Regulation.[360] As has been noted previously, under section 167 of the DPA 2018,

355. *See also* Art. 78(2) of the UK GDPR.
356. *Bright Jemwa v. Information Commissioner* [2021] UKFTT 2021_0278 (GRC) (22 Nov. 2021).
357. *See also Platts v. Information Commissioner* (EA/2018/0211/GDPR).
358. *See Scranage v. Information Commissioner* [2020] UKUT 196 (AAC).
359. *See Leighton v. Information Commissioner (No.2)* [2020] UKUT 23 (AAC).
360. *See* s. 167 of the DPA 2018. Note that the compliance orders do not include Part 4 DPA 2018.

the remedy sought for by the data subject is made without prejudice to other judicial or administrative remedies, including an action for damages under section 168 of the DPA 2018. This section applies if, on an application by a data subject, a court is satisfied that there has been an infringement of the data subject's rights under the data protection legislation in contravention of that legislation. Where an action is successful, the court may issue a compliance order.[361] The court may, for example, make an order for the purposes of securing compliance with the data protection legislation which requires the controller in respect of the processing, or a processor acting on behalf of that controller to either take steps specified in the order, or to refrain from taking steps specified in the order.[362]

§3. Representative Actions

174. Both the UK GDPR and the DPA 2018 make provision for representative actions to be brought on behalf of the data subject. Article 80 of the UK GDPR, for example, provides data subjects with a statutory right for representative actions if the conditions set out in section 187(3) and (4) of the DPA 2018 Act are met.[363] Data subjects have the right to mandate a body or other organisation which meets the conditions to lodge the complaint on his or her behalf, to exercise the rights referred to in Articles 77, 78 and 79 on his or her behalf, and to exercise the right to receive compensation referred to in Article 82 on his or her behalf.[364] Article 80 inserts into the provision the power of the Secretary of State to authorise relevant bodies, organisations or associations, independently of a data subject's mandate, to lodge a complaint with the Commissioner and to exercise the rights set out in Articles 78 and 79 if it considers that the rights of a data subject under this Regulation have been infringed as a result of the processing.[365]

175. Section 187 of the DPA 2018 sets out the framework governing the representation of data subjects with their authority. The right to authorise representation is in relation to the processing of personal data to which the UK GDPR applies. For example, the right applies to authorising a body or other organisation which meets the conditions set out in Article 80(1) of the UK GDPR to exercise the data subject's rights under Articles 77, 78 and 79 of the GDPR (rights to lodge complaints and to an effective judicial remedy) and to seek compensation on behalf the data

361. Section 167 of the DPA 2018.
362. Section 167(2) of the DPA 2018.
363. Note also Art. 55 of the Law Enforcement Directive.
364. Words in Art. 80(1) substituted (31.12.2020) by The Data Protection, Privacy and Electronic Communications (Amendments etc) (EU Exit) Regulations 2019 (S.I. 2019/419), reg. 1(2), Sch. 1 para. 59(2)(a) (with reg. 5); 2020 c. 1, Sch. 5 para. 1(1).
365. Article 80(3) inserted (31.12.2020) by The Data Protection, Privacy and Electronic Communications (Amendments etc) (EU Exit) Regulations 2019 (S.I. 2019/419), reg. 1(2), Sch. 1 para. 59(4) (with reg. 5); 2020 c. 1, Sch. 5 para. 1(1). Before the powers can be exercised by the Secretary of State, the requirements set out in s. 190 of the DPA 2018 must be met.

subject under Article 82 of the GDPR. It will be noted that the reference to authorising representative actions in respect of Articles 80(1) and 82 means that processing carried out by law enforcement authorities and intelligences services are not covered.

176. Section 187(2) of the DPA 2018 states that where processing of personal data is not covered by the UK GDPR, representative actions are still permitted for a narrow group of rights if two conditions are met.[366] The first condition to be met is that the body or organisation authorised by the data subject is required (after payment of outgoings) to apply the whole of its income, and any capital it expends for charitable or public purposes, is prohibited from directly or indirectly distributing amongst its members any part of its assets (otherwise than for charitable or public purposes), and has objectives which are in the public interest. The second condition is that the body or organisation is active in the field of protection of data subjects' rights and freedoms with regard to the protection of their personal data. If the Commissioner and/or Courts determine that both conditions are met, the representative action is available only in respect of lodging complaints with the Information Commissioner, requesting an order to progress complaints, seeking a compliance order, commencing judicial review proceedings against the Information Commissioner. Both the DPA 2018 and UK GDPR do not provide any guidance on how the discretion to investigate the complaint is to be exercised. The Information Commissioner has expressed the view that the exercise of the discretion should be informed by the overarching goals of enhancing public trust and promoting greater compliance:[367]

> The complaints the ICO receives from the public, including civil society, are crucial to helping us develop a rich picture of the information rights landscape. We can identify sectoral trends, multiple complaints about a controller, identify data breaches or where there has been suspected poor compliance. As a result, our guidance, investigation and enforcement work can be targeted in the right areas which benefit the public and encourage better compliance.
>
> We have therefore concentrated resources on the investigation of cases aimed at improving data security practices, reducing unlawful access, and addressing compliance concerns about the use of new surveillance technology. These areas, along with nuisance calls and texts, are a key focus of our investigative and enforcement activities.

---

366. Amendments in s. 187(1) made (31.12.2020) by virtue of The Data Protection, Privacy and Electronic Communications (Amendments etc) (EU Exit) Regulations 2019 (S.I. 2019/419), reg. 1(2), Sch. 2 para. 81(2) (with reg. 5); 2020 c. 1, Sch. 5 para. 1(1).

367. *See* The Information Commissioner's Office response to the Department for Digital, Culture, Media and Sport's Call for views and evidence – Review of Representative Action Provisions, Section 189 Data Protection Act 2018 (October 2020) Available at: https://ico.org.uk/about-the-ico/consultations/ico-response-to-dcms-review-of-representative-action-provisions/.

§4. Representative Actions: Collective Proceedings

177. Section 188 of the DPA 2018 provides the Secretary of State with the power to make regulations permitting collective proceedings, in relation to representative actions authorised by data subjects before a court or tribunal in England and Wales or Northern Ireland.[368] For example, the Secretary of State can make provision about proceedings combining an application to have personal data deleted (owing to the purposes for which the data collected has expired) with an application for compensation for material damage. Provision can also be made to confer functions on a person, including functions involving the exercise of a discretion. More specifically the power includes making provision in respect of the effect of judgments and orders; agreements to settle claims; the assessment of the amount of compensation; the persons to whom compensation may or must be paid, including compensation not claimed by the data subject; and costs. The power to make regulations under section 188 of the DPA 2018 is subject to a negative resolution procedure.[369]

§5. Representative Actions: Looking Ahead

178. The Department of Digital, Culture, Media and Sport issued a consultation on representative actions on 27 August 2020.[370] The consultation exercise and scope of the review were determined by fulfilling the mandate outlined in section 189 of the DPA 2018, which was to consider and report on matters such as the operation of section 187 of the DPA 2018, the merits of exercising the power under Article 80(2) of the UK GDPR, the need for an equivalent provision in relation to data subjects' rights under Article 82 of the GDPR (right to compensation), and the merits of making provision for a children's rights organisation to exercise some or all of a data subject's rights under Articles 77, 78, 79 and 82 of the UK GDPR on behalf of a data subject who is a child, with or without being authorised to do so by the data subject. The government received 345 written responses from organisations and individuals. Views were sought from privacy rights campaigners, organisations representing children and parents, academics, groups, trade associations, individual businesses and regulators. DCMS officials also engaged with the children and youth groups in Manchester and in London. A key issue arising from the consultation was whether there was a real public interest to be served by enacting new legislation to enable non-profit organisations to initiate complaints to the ICO or launch legal proceedings against data controllers on behalf of individuals unable to represent themselves. While privacy and organisations representing children were in favour of new legislation, business groups expressed concern that the creation of new avenues for litigation could be counterproductive. Though the issue of merits for embedding the right to respective actions in law is far from resolved, it seems that, at present, the

368. Section 188(1) and (2) of the DPA 2018.
369. Section 188(5) of the DPA 2018.
370. *See* https://www.gov.uk/government/publications/call-for-views-and-evidence-review-of-representative-action-provisions-section-189-data-protection-act-2018/uk-government-response-to-call-for-views-and-evidence-review-of-representative-action-provisions-section-189-data-protection-act-2018.

preferred regulatory response has been to use codes to facilitate more participatory engagement. The introduction of the Age Appropriate Design Code and utilisation of the civil procedure rules, as seen in *Lloyds v. Google*,[371] should go the way towards allaying concerns raised by non-profit organisations.[372]

371. UKSC 2019/0213 paras 84–89.
372. Note also the post-review powers to make provision about representation of data subjects under s. 190 of the DPA 2018.

Chapter 5. Liabilities

179. Article 82 of the UK GDPR states that any person who has suffered material or non-material damage as a result of an infringement of his or her rights under the Regulation shall have the right to receive compensation from the controller or processor for the damage suffered. Compensation for contravention of requirements of data protection legislation other than the GDPR is governed by section 169 of the DPA 2018.

180. The right to compensation under Article 82 and section 169 of the DPA 2018 can be enforced against any controller or processor.[373] It is worth noting the levels of attributions of liability to controllers and processors. A controller will be liable for any damage to the individual caused by processing.[374] The liability of a processor for the damage caused by processing will arise if it is shown that obligations under the GDPR specifically directed to processors have not been complied with or where the processor has acted outside or contrary to the lawful instructions of the controller.[375] Clearly, either a controller or processor will be exempt from liability if it is shown that it is not in any way responsible for the event giving rise to the damage. It is not sufficient to offer by way of defence to a claim for compensation under Article 82 or section 169, to argue that care was taken as was reasonably required to comply with the requirement concerned.[376] With regard to joint and several responsibility, Article 82(4) of the UK GDPR provides that where controllers and processors are involved in the same processing, they remain responsible for any damage caused by processing and are held liable for the entire damage in order to ensure effective compensation of the data subject. The only exemption available is when evidence is produced which proves that the controller or processor is not in any way responsible for the event giving rise to the damage.[377] In the event that the court issues an order that the controller pays the data subject full compensation for the damage suffered, Article 82(5) of the UK GDPR, it may claim back from the other controllers or processors involved in the same processing that part of the compensation corresponding to their part of responsibility for the damage. Interestingly, section 169 of the DPA 2018 is silent on the issue with regard to reclaiming monies from other controllers or processors.[378]

§1. Type of Damages

181. Article 82(1) of the UK GDPR provides that compensation is available for ‘material and non-material damage’. Section 168(1) of the DPA 2018 states that

373. Article 82(6) omitted (31.12.2020) by virtue of The Data Protection, Privacy and Electronic Communications (Amendments etc.) (EU Exit) Regulations 2019 (S.I. 2019/419), reg. 1(2), Sch. 1 para. 61 (with reg. 5, Sch. 1 para. 80); 2020 c. 1, Sch. 5 para. 1(1).
374. Article 82(2) of the UK GDPR and s. 169(2)(a) of the DPA 2018.
375. Article 82(2) of the UK GDPR and s. 169(2)(b) of the DPA 2018.
376. *See* as example the wording in s. 13(3) of the DPA 1998.
377. Article 82(2)(3) of the UK GDPR.
378. *See* s. 169(4) of the DPA 2018.

'non-material damage' includes distress. Section 169(5) of the DPA 2018, which applies to contravention of data protection legislation other than the GDPR, provides a non-exhaustive definition of 'damage'. 'Damage' includes financial loss and damage not involving financial loss, such as distress.

182. Reference should also be made to Recital 146, which gives us an indication of how the concept of 'damage' is to be understood in light of the interpretive section in section 168(1) of the DPA 2018:

> The concept of damage should be broadly interpreted in the light of the case-law of the Court of Justice in a manner which fully reflects the objectives of this Regulation. This is without prejudice to any claims for damage deriving from the violation of other rules in Union or Member State law. Processing that infringes this Regulation also includes processing that infringes delegated and implementing acts adopted in accordance with this Regulation and Member State law specifying rules of this Regulation. Data subjects should receive full and effective compensation for the damage they have suffered.

183. In *Lloyd v. Google*[379] a representative action was brought by the claimant under CPR 19.6. Damages were claimed under three categories: (i) the infringement of data protection rights; (ii) the commission of the wrong; and (iii) loss of control over personal data. No material loss or damage was alleged resulting from the use by Google of cookie software to override the Apple browser. Section 13 of the DPA 1998 provides that:

> (1) An individual who suffers damage by reason of any contravention by a data controller of any of the requirements of this Act is entitled to compensation from the data controller for that damage.
> (2) An individual who suffers distress by reason of any contravention by a data controller of any of the requirements of this Act is entitled to compensation from the data controller for that distress if:
> (a) the individual also suffers damage by reason of the contravention; or
> (b) the contravention relates to the processing of personal data for special purposes.
> (3) In proceedings brought against a person by virtue of this section it is a defence to prove that he had taken such care as in all the circumstances was reasonably required to comply with the requirement concerned.

184. The claim was dismissed at first instance by Mr Justice Warby holding that the claims under the three categories did not provide a legal basis for seeking compensation under section 13 of the DPA 1998.[380] The claim was however accepted on appeal. The Court of Appeal gave particular weight to the principle emerging in *Gulati v. MGN* that misuse of private information was a type of non-pecuniary loss

379. [2018] EWHC 2599 (QB).
380. Paragraphs 40–42 and 54–81.

that should give rise to legal redress.[381] Leave to appeal to the Supreme Court was granted on March 2020, and the decision was handed down on 10 November 2021.[382] The Supreme Court, by a unanimous decision, confirmed that a legal basis for damages required proof of distress or financial loss. Loss of control in itself was not deemed to be actionable. Lord Leggatt in delivering the leading judgment observed that:[383]

> In order to recover compensation under the DPA 1998 for any given individual, it would be necessary to show both that Google made some unlawful use of personal data relating to that individual and that the individual suffered some damage as a result. The claimant's attempt to recover compensation under the Act without proving either matter in any individual case is therefore doomed to fail.

185. When interpreting the scope of an actionable damage for the purposes of compensation under data protection law, the Supreme Court provided further guidance:[384]

> Two initial points can be made about the wording and structure of section 13. First, to recover compensation under this provision it is not enough to prove a breach by a data controller of its statutory duty under section 4(4) of the Act: an individual is only entitled to compensation under section 13 where 'damage' – or in some circumstances 'distress' – is suffered as a consequence of such a breach of duty. Second, it is plain from subsection (2) that the term 'damage' as it is used in section 13 does not include 'distress'. The term 'material damage' is sometimes used to describe any financial loss or physical or psychological injury, but excluding distress (or other negative emotions not amounting to a recognised psychiatric illness): see eg Watkins v Secretary of State for the Home Department [2006] UKHL 17; [2006] 2 AC 395, para 7. Adopting this terminology, on a straightforward interpretation the term 'damage' in section 13 refers only to material damage and compensation can only be recovered for distress if either of the two conditions set out in subsection (2) is met.

186. It should be made clear that where there are possible sub-processors and joint controllers, any issue about apportioning blame or level of compensation as between the controllers and processors will not have an impact on the right to compensation.[385]

---

381. [2019] EWCA Civ 1599. *Gulati v. MGN Limited* [2015] EWHC 1482 (Ch). *See also Halliday v. Creation Consumer Finance Limited* [2013] EWCA Civ 333 (unauthorised processing of personal data) and *Weller v. Associated Newspapers Ltd* [2014] EMLR 24 (damages for misuse of photographs of children).
382. [2021] UKSC 50.
383. Paragraph 8.
384. *Ibid.*, para. 92.
385. *See*, for example, *Various Claimants v. WM Morrison Supermarket* [2018] EWCA 2239.

Chapter 6. Penalties

187. The Information Commissioner is the supervisory authority for the UK, as provided for by Article 51 of the UK GDPR.[386] By Article 57(1) of the UK GDPR, it is the Information Commissioner's task to monitor and enforce the application of the GDPR. By Article 58(2)(d) of the UK GDPR, the Information Commissioner has the power to notify controllers of alleged infringements of GDPR. The Information Commissioner is responsible for monitoring the application of UK GDPR, as provided for by Articles 51 and 57(1)(a) of the UK GDPR. Under Article 58(2)(i) of the UK GDPR, the Information Commissioner has the power to impose an administrative fine, in accordance with Article 83, in addition to or instead of the other corrective measures referred to in Article 58(2) of the UK GDPR, depending on the circumstances of each individual case.

188. To this end, the Information Commissioner is provided with enforcement powers under the GDPR. The DPA 2018 contains various enforcement powers in Part 6 which are exercisable by the Information Commissioner. The matters identified in Article 83(2)(a)–(k) of the UK GDPR are also set out in section 155(3) of the DPA 2018 and are generally referred to as 'the Statutory Factors'. These powers are also complemented by additional enforcement provisions under the PECR 2003 and the Freedom of Information Act 2000 (FOIA 2000).[387]

189. Section 155 of the DPA 2018 vests in the Information Commissioner the power to issue a written penalty notice, requiring the person to pay a specified amount. Under Part 6 of the DPA 2018, there are two tiers of penalty for an infringement of data protection rules – a higher maximum and a standard maximum. The higher maximum amount is GPB 17.5 million or 4% of the total annual worldwide turnover in the preceding financial year, whichever is higher. The decision to issue the higher maximum amount is not limited to egregious violations. The Information Commissioner has indicated that a higher maximum monetary penalty notice amount can also be issued in respect of a failure to comply with any of the data protection principles, any rights an individual may have under Part 3 of the DPA 2018 or in relation to any cross-border transfers of data to third countries. As a rule of thumb infringements akin to non-compliance with, for example, administrative requirements of data protection rules, the standard maximum amount will apply, which currently is GBP 8.7 million or 2% of the total annual worldwide turnover in the preceding financial year, whichever is higher.

---

386. Words in Art. 51(1) substituted (31.12.2020) by The Data Protection, Privacy and Electronic Communications (Amendments etc) (EU Exit) Regulations 2019 (S.I. 2019/419), reg. 1(2), Sch. 1 para. 45(3)(a) (with reg. 5); 2020 c. 1, Sch. 5 para. 1(1). Sub-sections (2) to (4) in Art. 51 omitted (31.12.2020) by virtue of The Data Protection, Privacy and Electronic Communications (Amendments etc) (EU Exit) Regulations 2019 (S.I. 2019/419), reg. 1(2), Sch. 1 para. 45(4) (with reg. 5, Sch. 1 para. 80); 2020 c. 1, Sch. 5 para. 1(1).
387. Note also the Network and Information Systems Regulations 2018, the EU Electronic Identification, Authentication and Trust Services Regulation, the Environmental Information Regulations 2004, the Re-use of Public Sector Information Regulations 2015 and the INSPIRE Regulations 2009.

190. When serving the penalty notice, the Information Commissioner is required to have regard to the matters listed in Article 83(1) and (2) of the UK GDPR. When making a determination of whether a monetary penalty notice is to be issued, the Commissioner can also take into account the categories of personal data affected by the failure; the damage and distress suffered by data subjects; the manner in which the infringement became known to the Information Commissioner, including whether, and if so to what extent, the controller or processor notified the Information Commissioner of the failure; the extent to which the controller or processor has complied with previous enforcement notices or penalty notices; adherence to approved codes of conduct or certification mechanisms; the culpability of the controller or processor; any other aggravating or mitigating factor applicable to the case, including financial benefits gained, or losses avoided, as a result of the failure (whether directly or indirectly); whether the penalty would be effective, proportionate and dissuasive.

191. For example, the Information Commissioner decided to issue a controller ('Tuckers Solicitors LLP') with a Penalty Notice under section 155 of the DPA 2018.[388] Tuckers Solicitors LLP was fined GBP 98,000. The facts can be briefly stated. On 24 August 2020, Tuckers Solicitors LLP's computing systems were subjected to a ransomware attack. A personal data breach notification was made to the Information Commissioner on 25 August 2020 after internal investigations revealed the ransomware attack had compromised computing system. Even though the attack was limited to the archive server, the Information Commissioner considered the failure to implement appropriate technical and organisation measures over some or all of the relevant period rendered it vulnerable to the attack. The volume of personal data compromised by encryption was not negligible. Out of the 972,191 individual files encrypted, 24,712 were related to court bundles. From this group of encrypted bundles, 60 were exfiltrated by the attacker and released in underground data marketplaces. The compromised files included both personal data and special category data. The Information Commissioner also noted that there were other compliance violations, notably with Articles 5(1)(e), 25, 32(l)(a) and 32(l)(b) of the UK GDPR – but these did not form the basis of the monetary penalty notice. The Information Commissioner concluded that the controller failed to process personal data in a manner that ensured appropriate security of the personal data, including protection against unauthorised or unlawful processing and against accidental loss, destruction or damage, using appropriate technical or organisational measures. The reasoning informing the decision to impose an administrative fine can be gleaned from the notice issued by the Information Commissioner:

> Taking into consideration the highly sensitive nature of the personal data that Tuckers were processing, as well as the state of the security updates, and the costs of implementation for them, Tuckers should not have been processing personal data on an infrastructure containing known critical vulnerabilities

388. The penalty notice imposes an administrative fine on Tuckers, in accordance with the Commissioner's powers under Art. 83 of the UK GDPR. Available at https://ico.org.uk/action-weve-taken/enforcement/tuckers-solicitors-llp-mpn/.

without appropriately addressing the risk. In doing so, it did not ensure appropriate security, including protection against unauthorised and unlawful processing of its personal data, as required by Article S(l)(f) GDPR ... The personal data included within the bundles included special category data, and related to individuals that were particularly vulnerable, including children and individuals involved in significant crimes. This, in the Commissioner's view, increases the severity of this infringement, given that this type of personal data required particularly high levels of security to be applied to it. In terms of the assessment of damage suffered by affected data subjects, the Commissioner has regard to Recital 85 GDPR which explains that 'physical, material or non-material damage to natural persons such as loss of control over their personal data or limitation of their rights, discrimination, identity theft or fraud, financial loss, unauthorised reversal of pseudonymisation, damage to reputation, loss of confidentiality of personal data protected by professional secrecy or any other significant economic or social disadvantage to the natural person concerned'.

192. The procedures for issuing a monetary penalty notice are set out in the DPA 2018. A penalty notice can be served on any person or organisation that has failed to comply with an information notice, an assessment notice or an enforcement notice. A penalty notice can also be issued by the Information Commissioner if a person has failed to comply with the provisions in section 149(2)–(5) of the DPA 2018. Monetary penalties come under four categories. The first category involves the failure of a controller or processor to comply with their obligations under the UK GDPR, such as non-compliance with fair processing principles under Article 5, violation of the rights conferred on a data subject (e.g., Articles 17, 18, 21 and 22), fulfilling the transparency and accountability obligations (e.g., Articles 12, 13, 14 and 15), communicating to the Commissioner or data subject a personal data breach (e.g., Articles 32, 33, and 34) and principles governing the transfer of personal data to third countries, non-Convention countries and international organisations (e.g., Articles 44, 45, 46 and 47). The next category comprises the failure of a body to comply with an obligation under Article 41 of the UK GDPR, with regard to monitoring approved codes of conduct. Failures by certification providers come within the third category which can be the subject of a penalty notice. The penalty notice is directed at the failure by the certification provider to meet the requirements for accreditation or non-compliance with obligation under Article 42 or 43 of the UK GDPR or non-compliance with any other provision of the UK GDPR whether in the person's capacity as a certification provider or otherwise). The final category involves failure by a controller to pay charges as required by the Information Commissioner under section 137 of the DPA 2018.

§1. Section 160 of the DPA 2018: Regulatory Action Policy

193. Under the DPA 2018, the Commissioner is under a duty to produce and publish guidance about how the Commissioner proposes to exercise the Commissioner's functions in connection with the following: information notices, assessment notices, enforcement notices, and penalty notices. The ICO consultation on the draft Regulatory Action Policy closed on 24th March 2022, and guidance is available on the website.[389]

389. *See* https://ico.org.uk/about-the-ico/ico-and-stakeholder-consultations/ico-consultation-on-the-draft-rap-statutory-guidance-on-our-regulatory-action-and-statutory-guidance-on-our-pecr-powers/. Also ICO DRAFT Regulatory action policy 2021 (https://ico.org.uk/media/about-the-ico/consultations/4019212/regulatory-action-policy-2021-for-consultation.pdf) and ICO, *See also* EDPB, Guidelines 01/2021 on Examples regarding Personal Data Breach Notification (2021). Adopted on 14 Dec. 2021 Version 2.0.

Part IX. Specific Processing Situations

Chapter 1. Processing for Journalistic Purposes and Academic, Artistic or Literary Expression

194. Freedom of expression, whether it is in an academic, artistic or literary situation or for journalistic purposes, is protected by Article 11 of the EU Charter of Fundamental Rights ('Freedom of expression and information'). This right is understood in very broad terms to include the 'freedom to hold opinions and to receive and impart information and ideas without interference by public authority and regardless of frontiers'. The freedom of expression or the right to receive/impart information is not absolute. Limitations on the freedom of expression must comply with the criteria provided for in Article 52(1) of the Charter. Additionally, Article 11 corresponds with Article 10 of the ECHR which states that pursuant to Article 52(3) of the Charter, insofar as it contains rights that correspond to rights guaranteed by the ECHR, 'the meaning and scope of those rights shall be the same as those laid down by the said Convention'. Limits to the right guaranteed by Article 11 of the Charter must be prescribed by law, and be necessary in a democratic society 'for the protection [...] of the reputation or rights of others'. Such rights encompass, notably, the right to respect for private life and the right to personal data protection.

195. There is no statutory definition of the situations covered by the special purposes exemption under section 174 of the DPA 2018. In *Satamedia* the Grand Chamber outlined the reasoning process involved when making a determination of when the freedom of expression exemption becomes a live issue:[390]

> In order to take account of the importance of the right to freedom of expression in every democratic society, it is necessary, first, to interpret notions relating to that freedom, such as journalism, broadly. Secondly, and in order to achieve a balance between the two fundamental rights, the protection of the fundamental right to privacy requires that the derogations and limitations in relation to the protection of data provided for in the chapters of the directive referred to above must apply only in so far as is strictly necessary.

196. The ruling in *Axel Springer AG v. Germany* is illustrative of the considerations that need to be brought into play when reconciling both these sets of

390. C-73/07, C-73/07 – Satakunnan Markkinapörssi and Satamedia Judgment of the Court (Grand Chamber) 16 Dec. 2008, para. 56.

rights.[391] The journalist concerned interviewed relevant law enforcement personnel and a news feature recounting the arrest and conviction with photos of the well-known actor and published under the sensational headline – 'Cocaine! Superintendent Y caught at the Munich beer festival.' In holding that the applicant's Article 10 Convention rights had been violated, the ECtHR set out the considerations that need to be taken into account when balancing the right to freedom of expression against the right to respect for private life, as established in its case law: contribution to a debate of general interest, the status and/or identify of the person concerned (e.g., public figure) and subject of the report, the method of obtaining the information and its veracity, content, form and consequences of the impugned articles and severity of the sanction imposed on the applicant company.[392]

§1. The DPPEC Regulations and Special Purposes

197. Following the UK's departure from the EU, the Charter will cease to be available when determining the availability of the exemption in the domestic context.[393] Chapter IX of the UK GDPR contains some relevant exemptions to the processing of personal data for special purposes such as journalism, academic, artistic or literary expression. Article 85 of the EU GDPR requires the Member States to reconcile the right to the protection of personal data with the freedom of expression. There is no overriding duty to balance the interests under the DPA 2018 and UK GDPR. Article 85(1) is deleted, and the general obligation to reconcile the right to the protection of personal data with the rights to freedom of expression and information is removed by Article 85(2).[394] The Secretary of State is, however, under an obligation to provide for exemptions if they are necessary. Article 85(2A) requires the Secretary of State when exercising the power by making regulations under section 16 of the DPA 2018.

§2. The 'Special Purposes'

198. Section 174 of the DPA 2018 states that special purposes mean journalistic purposes; academic purposes; artistic purposes; or literary purposes. As the DPA 2018 provides no definition, these purposes are to be given their natural and ordinary meaning. The Commissioner has not provided any guidance on whether these

---

391. ECtHR, *Axel Springer AG v. Germany* [GC], No. 39954/08, 2012. *See also* ECtHR, *Coudec and Hachette Filipacchi Associés v. France* [GC], No. 40454/07, 10 Nov. 2015. Compare with ECtHR, *Delfi AS v. Estonia* [GC] No. 64569/09, *Wingrove v. UK* (1997) 24 EHRR 1 ('artistic' expression).
392. *Ibid.* paras 96–109.
393. However, note that data controllers and data processors whose activities or operations bring them within the scope of EU law, the GDPR and Charter will continue to be relevant.
394. For deletion of Art. 85(1) *see* The Data Protection, Privacy and Electronic Communications (Amendments etc) (EU Exit) Regulations 2019 (S.I. 2019/419), reg. 1(2), Sch. 1 para. 64(2) (with reg. 5, Sch. 1 para. 80); 2020 c. 1, Sch. 5 para. 1(1). The obligation in Art. 85(2) is replaced by Words in Art. 85(2) substituted (31.12.2020) by The Data Protection, Privacy and Electronic Communications (Amendments etc) (EU Exit) Regulations 2019 (S.I. 2019/419), reg. 1(2), Sch. 1 para. 64(3)(a) (with reg. 5); 2020 c. 1, Sch. 5 para. 1(1).

purposes can be regarded as being an inherent value of the freedom of expression.[395] One view, based on the approach adopted in *Satamedia*, is that the data subject's fundamental right to the protection of personal data must be balanced with an equally valuable fundamental right, namely the right to freedom of expression. The fact that journalism may be a commercial activity does not detract from the fact that journalistic activities such as disclosure to the public of information, opinion or ideas underline the importance of the right to freedom of expression in a democratic society.[396]

§3. UK EXEMPTIONS AND DEROGATIONS FOR JOURNALISTIC PURPOSES: PART 5, SCHEDULE II, DPA 18

199. The scope of the UK's exemptions for journalistic purposes is now set out in Part 5, Schedule II of the UK's DPA 2018. To be relieved of the obligations, the processing of personal data must be carried out with a view to the publication by a person of journalistic, academic, artistic or literary material, and the controller must hold a reasonable belief that the publication of the material would be in the public interest. In determining whether publication would be in the public interest the controller must take into account the special importance of the public interest in the freedom of expression and information. An important factor when determining that the belief that the publication would be in the public interest is reasonable, the controller must have regard to any of the following codes of practice or guidelines, relevant to the publication in question. These codes of practice or guidelines are the BBC Editorial Guidelines; Ofcom Broadcasting Code; Editors' Code of Practice and the Draft Code of Practice on Journalism.

200. Additionally, the controller must reasonably believe that the application of the listed UK GDPR provisions would be incompatible with the special purposes. For the purposes of the special purposes exemption, the controller will be relieved from complying with the following obligations under the provisions in the UK GDPR:[397]

(a) in Chapter II of the UK GDPR such as Article 5(1)(a) to (e) (principles relating to processing); Article 6 (lawfulness); Article 7 (conditions for consent); Article 8(1) and (2) (child's consent); Article 9 (processing of special categories of data); Article 10 (data relating to criminal convictions etc.); Article 11(2) (processing not requiring identification);

395. *See* https://ico.org.uk/for-organisations/guide-to-data-protection/guide-to-the-general-data-protection-regulation-gdpr/exemptions/#ex16 and ICO, Draft Journalism Code of Practice.
396. Satamedia paras 56–61.
397. Words in Sch. 2 para. 26(9) substituted (31.12.2020) by The Data Protection, Privacy and Electronic Communications (Amendments etc) (EU Exit) Regulations 2019 (S.I. 2019/419), reg. 1(2), Sch. 2 para. 92(21)(a) (b) (with reg. 5); 2020 c. 1, Sch. 5 para. 1(1).

(b) in Chapter III of the UK GDPR such as Article 13(1) to (3) (personal data collected from data subject: information to be provided); Article 14(1) to (4) (personal data collected other than from data subject: information to be provided); Article 15(1) to (3) (confirmation of processing, access to data and safeguards for third country transfers); Article 16 (right to rectification); Article 17(1) and (2) (right to erasure); Article 18(1)(a), (b) and (d) (restriction of processing); Article 19 (notification obligation regarding rectification or erasure of personal data or restriction of processing); Article 20(1) and (2) (right to data portability); Article 21(1) (objections to processing);
(c) in Chapter IV of the [F5UK GDPR] (controller and processor) such as Article 34(1) and (4) (communication of personal data breach to the data subject); Article 36 (requirement for controller to consult Commissioner prior to high-risk processing);
(d) in Chapter V of the UK GDPR (transfers of data to third countries etc.), Article 44 (general principles for transfers).

201. The Draft Journalism Code of Practice provides updated, relevant guidance. The consultation closed on 24 January 2022 and was initiated under section 124 of the DPA 2018.[398] The Draft Journalism code will be particularly relevant to those processing personal data for the purposes of journalism. Media organisations, freelancers and those engaged in blogging would find much useful guidance. The Draft Journalism Code has also been revised to include materials relevant to those in the legal profession, DPO and senior editorial staff. The ICO's guidance also gives particular importance to the maintaining of documentation which covers the conduct of DPIAs where the processing is likely to involve a higher risk. Controllers are also encouraged to maintain accurate records and where appropriate to consult with the Information Commissioner. Under Article 9(2)(g) of the UK GDPR, processing is exempted from data protections rules on the grounds that it is necessary for reasons of substantial public interest, to the extent that the processing is proportionate to the aim pursued, respects the essence of the right to data protection and provide for suitable and specific measures to safeguard the fundamental rights and the interests of the data subject.[399] Journalism in connection with disclosure of unlawful acts and dishonesty is deemed to meet the substantial public interest threshold if evidence is shown of the commission of an unlawful act by a person; dishonesty, malpractice or other seriously improper conduct of a person or unfitness or incompetence of a person. The substantial public interest processing is likely to be relevant in cases of whistleblowing and investigative journalism.

---

398. *See* https://ico.org.uk/about-the-ico/ico-and-stakeholder-consultations/ico-consultation-on-the-draft-journalism-code-of-practice/.
399. *See also* s. 10(1)(b) of the DPA 2018.

Chapter 2. Processing of Personal Information Versus Public Access to Official Documents

202. There are four regimes that relate to access to personal information held by public authorities: the FOIA 2000, the Freedom of Information (Scotland) Act 2002, Environmental Information Regulations 2004 (EIR) and INSPIRE Regulations.[400] The access regimes are designed to make provision for public access to official information, with a view to ensuring transparency and accountability in the public sector. Data protection law is specifically engaged by the FOIA as most information held by public authorities will include personal data. Access regimes are underpinned by the desire to promote open government. By way of contrast, data protection law aims to provide a regulatory framework that seeks to balance the interests between data subjects and data controllers on the one hand, and balancing the interests of data subjects (such as protection of their personal data and privacy) with other fundamental rights and interests. A related point is that much of regulatory framework provided by data protection law is concerned with the processing of personal data, which includes controllers and processors from the public and private sectors. Access regimes are concerned with the activities of public sector bodies and cover a wide range of information, and not limited to personal information. For example, the EIR regulates access to 'environmental information', which includes any information in written, visual, aural, electronic or any other form on the state of the elements of the environment, such as air and atmosphere, substances, or reports on the implementation of environmental legislation.[401] While access regimes are underpinned by the presumption of access, data protection law permits processing of personal data if there is a legal basis and is subjected to a number of fair processing principles. Both data protection and access regimes are also accompanied by exemptions.

§1. The DPPEC Regulations and Access Regimes

203. The DPPEC Regulations have made some amendments to the EU GDPR. Article 2(1A) of the UK GDPR states that the Regulation applies to the manual unstructured processing of personal data held by an FOI public authority.[402] This material is excluded under Article 2(a) and (b) under the EU GDPR. Under Article 2(5) of the UK GDPR an 'FOI public authority' will have the same meaning as in Chapter 3 of Part 2 of the 2018 Act (*see* section 21(5) of that Act).[403] References to

400. *See* https://ico.org.uk/your-data-matters/official-information/.
401. Regulation 2 The Environmental Information Regulations 2004 SI 2004/3391.
402. Article 2(1)(1A) substituted for Art. 2(1) (31.12.2020) by The Data Protection, Privacy and Electronic Communications (Amendments etc) (EU Exit) Regulations 2019 (S.I. 2019/419), reg. 1(2), Sch. 1 para. 4(2) (as amended by S.I. 2020/1586, regs 1(2), 4(2)) (with reg. 5); 2020 c. 1, Sch. 5 para. 1(1).
403. Article 2(5) inserted (31.12.2020) by The Data Protection, Privacy and Electronic Communications (Amendments etc) (EU Exit) Regulations 2019 (S.I. 2019/419), reg. 1(2), Sch. 1 para. 4(6) (with reg. 5); 2020 c. 1, Sch. 5 para. 1(1).

personal data held by an FOI public authority are to be interpreted in accordance with section 21(6) and (7) of the DPA 2018. Article 86(2) of the UK GDPR makes this change clear.[404]

204. Article 2(2) of the UK GDPR excludes the processing of personal data by a competent authority for any of the law enforcement purposes (*see* Part 3 of the 2018 Act).[405]

205. Following the UK's departure from the EU, public authorities faced with access requests will now turn to the general processing category in Part 2 of the DPA 2018. An authority or body that falls within the definition of public authority or public body under section 7 is regarded as such when performing a task carried out in the public interest or in the exercise of official authority vested in it.[406] Parish councils are excluded from this category and therefore not required to appoint a DPO.

206. The Secretary of State may by regulations provide that a person specified or described in the regulations that is a public authority described in subsection (1)(a) or (b) is not a 'public authority' or 'public body' for the purposes of the UK GDPR.[407]

207. Section 24 of the DPA 2018 contains a number of exemptions, which have been previously outside the material scope of the GDPR. Part 3 of the DPA 2018 now sets out provisions governing requests for access to processing undertaken for law enforcement purposes by competent authorities. Section 31 of the DPA 2018 defines 'law enforcement purposes' as comprising:

> purposes of the prevention, investigation, detection or prosecution of criminal offences or the execution of criminal penalties, including the safeguarding against and the prevention of threats to public security.

208. A public authority or body will be a 'competent body' if it comes under Schedule 7 DPA 2018. If the processing of personal data is not undertaken for the stated purposes, the relevant data subject's rights and principles under the DPA 2018

---

404. Article 86(2) inserted (31.12.2020) by The Data Protection, Privacy and Electronic Communications (Amendments etc) (EU Exit) Regulations 2019 (S.I. 2019/419), reg. 1(2), Sch. 1 para. 65(4) (with reg. 5); 2020 c. 1, Sch. 5 para. 1(1).
405. Article 2(2) substituted (31.12.2020) by The Data Protection, Privacy and Electronic Communications (Amendments etc) (EU Exit) Regulations 2019 (S.I. 2019/419), reg. 1(2), Sch. 1 para. 4(3) (with reg. 5); 2020 c. 1, Sch. 5 para. 1(1).
406. Words in s. 7(2) substituted (31.12.2020) by The Data Protection, Privacy and Electronic Communications (Amendments etc) (EU Exit) Regulations 2019 (S.I. 2019/419), reg. 1(2), Sch. 2 para. 10(3) (with reg. 5); 2020 c. 1, Sch. 5 para. 1(1).
407. Words in s. 7(4) substituted (31.12.2020) by The Data Protection, Privacy and Electronic Communications (Amendments etc) (EU Exit) Regulations 2019 (S.I. 2019/419), reg. 1(2), Sch. 2 para. 10(3) (with reg. 5); 2020 c. 1, Sch. 5 para. 1(1). The regulations will be subject to an affirmative resolution procedure.

will come into operation. Finally, Intelligence Services are exempt from FOIA and references to be made to Part 4 of the DPA 2018.

209. Article 85(1) which requires the law to 'reconcile the right to the protection of personal data pursuant to this Regulation with the right to freedom of expression and information' has been removed.[408] Article 85(2) of the UK GDPR now provides the Secretary of State with the power to issue derogations and derogations, but it is not entirely clear whether it is in the context of specific data processing situations (processing for journalistic purposes and the purposes of academic, artistic or literary expression) in Chapter IX rather than access regimes such as FOI.[409]

§2. Public Authorities, Personal Data and Access

210. As noted in previous chapters, public authorities will be controllers when processing personal data. The broad definition of 'personal data' will include all information relating to individuals held by the public authority, as well as any correspondence arising from services provided to the community.

211. The Information Commissioner has issued comprehensive guidance on access requests made to public authorities with regard to information held. As a general rule, public authorities will need to consider carefully their obligations under Chapters III and IV of the UK GDPR and the general processing category in Chapter 2 of Part 2 of the DPA 2018. Given that processing of manual unstructured data is now covered, public authorities will need to take account of Chapter 3 and applicable provisions in UK GDPR. Particular attention needs to be given to the legal basis for processing under Article 6 of the UK GDPR. For example, processing by a public authority can be justified on the basis that it is necessary for the performance of a task carried out in the public interest or in the exercise of official authority vested in the controller'.[410] When publishing information processed, public authorities need to comply with the provisions under the UK GDPR and DPA 2018 as appropriate. Care needs to be taken where access requests are made by the public in respect of special categories of information. Such information cannot be released unless the information is already available in the public domain.

212. With regard to access requests for manual unstructured processing operations undertaken by public authorities, section 24 of the DPA 2018 provides a broad

408. Article 85(1) omitted (31.12.2020) by virtue of The Data Protection, Privacy and Electronic Communications (Amendments etc) (EU Exit) Regulations 2019 (S.I. 2019/419), reg. 1(2), Sch. 1 para. 64(2) (with reg. 5, Sch. 1 para. 80); 2020 c. 1, Sch. 5 para. 1(1).

409. Words in Art. 85(2) substituted (31.12.2020) by The Data Protection, Privacy and Electronic Communications (Amendments etc) (EU Exit) Regulations 2019 (S.I. 2019/419), reg. 1(2), Sch. 1 para. 64(3)(b) (with reg. 5); 2020 c. 1, Sch. 5 para. 1(1) and those omitted (31.12.2020) by virtue of The Data Protection, Privacy and Electronic Communications (Amendments etc) (EU Exit) Regulations 2019 (S.I. 2019/419), reg. 1(2), Sch. 1 para. 64(3)(c) (with reg. 5, Sch. 1 para. 80); 2020 c. 1, Sch. 5 para. 1(1).

410. Article 6(1)(e) of the UK GDPR.

list of exemptions, which effectively disapply many of the data processing principles and rights. Under section 24(5), the public authority is not obliged to comply with Article 15(1) to (3) of the UK GDPR (right of access by the data subject) in relation to personal data to which the UK GDPR applies by virtue Article 2(1A) if the request under Article 15 does not contain a description of the personal data, or the controller estimates that the cost of complying with the request so far as relating to the personal data would exceed the appropriate maximum.

213. Finally, there are special exemptions for personal data under the access regime which should not be overlooked. First, an application by a data subject should be made under the data protection rather than the access regime provided by the FOIA. Second, where the FOIA is relied upon to gain access to personal data of a third party, an assessment has to be made with regard to its publication by the application of data protection principles.[411] For example, when a request is made by a third party, the public authority will have to take into account whether the data subject will be entitled to exercise the rights to restriction or objection under Articles 18 or 21 of the UK GDPR.[412]

214. Finally reference should be made to paragraph 58 Schedule 19 DPA 2018 which amends section 40 FOIA in some material respects:

> (3A) The first condition is that the disclosure of the information to a member of the public otherwise than under this Act –
> (a) would contravene any of the data protection principles; or
> (b) would do so if the exemptions in section 24(1) of the Data Protection Act 2018 (manual unstructured data held by public authorities) were disregarded.
> (3B) The second condition is that the disclosure of the information to a member of the public otherwise than under this Act would contravene Article 21 of the GDPR (general processing: right to object to processing).
> (4) For subsection (4) substitute –
> (4A) The third condition is that –
> (a) on a request under Article 15(1) of the GDPR (general processing: right of access by the data subject) for access to personal data, the information would be withheld in reliance on provision made by or under section 15, 16 or 26 of, or Schedule 2, 3 or 4 to, the Data Protection Act 2018; or
> (b) on a request under section 45(1)(b) of that Act (law enforcement processing: right of access by the data subject), the information would be withheld in reliance on subsection (4) of that section.‘

411. *Lewis v. Secretary of State for Health* [2008] EWHC 2196 (QB) (duty of confidence) and *Queen Mary University of London v. IC and Matthees* EA/2015/0269, 12 Aug. 2016 (patient level data and identifiability).
412. Corporate Officer of the *House of Commons v. IC and Norman Baker* EA/2006/0015 and 0016, 16 Jan. 2007 (MPs travel expenses), *Rob Waugh v. IC and Doncaster College* EA/2008/0038, 24 Dec. 2008 (internal disciplinary matters) and *DH v. IC* [2016] UKUT 139 (AAC) (default of council tax by public official).

(5) For subsection (5) substitute –

(5A) The duty to confirm or deny does not arise in relation to information which is (or if it were held by the public authority would be) exempt information by virtue of subsection (1).

(5B) The duty to confirm or deny does not arise in relation to other information if or to the extent that any of the following applies –

(a) giving a member of the public the confirmation or denial that would have to be given to comply with section 1(1)(a) –
   (i) would (apart from this Act) contravene any of the data protection principles; or
   (ii) would do so if the exemptions in section 24(1) of the Data Protection Act 2018 (manual unstructured data held by public authorities) were disregarded;

(b) giving a member of the public the confirmation or denial that would have to be given to comply with section 1(1)(a) would (apart from this Act) contravene Article 21 of the GDPR (general processing: right to object to processing);

(c) on a request under Article 15(1) of the GDPR (general processing: right of access by the data subject) for confirmation of whether personal data is being processed, the information would be withheld in reliance on a provision listed in subsection (4A)(a);

(d) on a request under section 45(1)(a) of the Data Protection Act 2018 (law enforcement processing: right of access by the data subject), the information would be withheld in reliance on subsection (4) of that section.

(7) For subsection (7) substitute –

(7) In this section –

'the data protection principles' means the principles set out in –

(a) Article 5(1) of the GDPR, and

(b) section 34(1) of the Data Protection Act 2018;

'data subject' has the same meaning as in the Data Protection Act 2018 (*see* section 3 of that Act);

'the GDPR', 'personal data', 'processing' and references to a provision of Chapter 2 of Part 2 of the Data Protection Act 2018 have the same meaning as in Parts 5 to 7 of that Act (*see* section 3(2), (4), (10), (11) and (14) of that Act).

(8)In determining for the purposes of this section whether the lawfulness principle in Article 5(1)(a) of the GDPR would be contravened by the disclosure of information, Article 6(1) of the GDPR (lawfulness) is to be read as if the second sub-paragraph (disapplying the legitimate interests gateway in relation to public authorities) were omitted.

215. The exemption from the duty to confirm or deny is one which has attracted some interest (Non-Circumvention and Non-Disclosure (NCND)). The NCND can be particularly problematic as any statement, which either confirms or denies that particular information is or is not held can be used to draw inferences and potentially revealing. In *Larry Simons v. IC* the London Borough of Barnet received a request requiring confirmation that complaints had been made about a particular individual. The First Tier Tribunal held that confirming or denying would involve processing of personal data and reveal, in this case, highly sensitive information which identified the individual.[413]

413. *Larry Simons v. IC* EA/2013/0254, 4 Apr. 2014. *See also Goodall v. ICO* EA/2014/0074, 30 Sep. 2014.

Chapter 3. Processing of the National Identification Number

216. The DPA 2018 has omitted Article 87 of the GDPR on the processing of national identification number.[414]

414. Schedule 6 para. 60 to DPA 2018.

Chapter 4. Processing in the Context of Employment

217. The DPA 2018 has omitted Article 88 of the GDPR regarding processing in the context of employment.[415]

415. Schedule 6 para. 61 to DPA 2018.

Chapter 5. Processing for Scientific Research, Public Archiving and Statistical Purposes

218. Article 89 of the UK GDPR follows Article 89 of the GDPR and allows for certain exemptions when personal data are processed for archiving purposes in the public interest, scientific or historical research purposes or statistical purposes. Insofar as research and statistics are concerned, exemptions are allowed regarding confirmation of processing and access to data and safeguards for third country transfers (Article 15(1) and (3) of the UK GDPR); right to rectification (Article 16 of the UK GDPR); restriction of processing (Article 18(1) of the UK GDPR) and objection to processing (Article 21(1) of the UK GDPR).[416] The exceptions to these provisions are permitted for scientific, historical research or statistical purposes to the extent that the application of those provisions would prevent or seriously impair the achievement of these purposes.[417]

219. Insofar as archiving in the public interest is concerned, exemptions are possible in the above cases as well as for the notification obligation regarding rectification or erasure of personal data or restriction of processing (Article 19 of the UK GDPR) and to the right to data portability (Article 20(1) of the UK GDPR).[418] These exceptions are allowed for archiving purposes in the public interest to the extent that the application of those provisions would prevent or seriously impair the achievement of those purposes.[419]

416. Schedule 2 Part 6 para. 27(2) to DPA 2018.
417. Schedule 2 Part 6 para. 27(1) to DPA 2018.
418. Schedule 2 Part 6 para. 28(2) to DPA 2018.
419. Schedule 2 Part 6 para. 28(1) to DPA 2018.

Part X. Specific Data Protection Regimes

Chapter 1. Obligations of Professional Secrecy (Including Equivalent Obligations of Secrecy)

220. Article 90 of the EU GDPR vests in supervisory authorities the power to develop rules with regard to securing:

> an obligation of professional secrecy or other equivalent obligations of secrecy where this is necessary and proportionate to reconcile the right of the protection of personal data with the obligation of secrecy.

221. The specialised data protection regime only applies 'with regard to personal data which the controller or processor has received as a result of or has obtained in an activity covered by that obligation of secrecy'.

222. Even though the DPPEC Regulations have omitted Article 90, there are a number of exemptions under the DPA 2018 and UK GDPR that lend themselves to enhancing obligations of professional secrecy.[420] The following accounts of specific data protection regimes are provided for illustration purposes only.

§1. Obligations of Secrecy and Sensitive Data

223. Articles 9(2)(h) and (i) of the UK GDPR provide as follows:[421]

> processing is necessary for the purposes of preventive or occupational medicine, for the assessment of the working capacity of the employee, medical diagnosis, the provision of health or social care or treatment or the management of health or social care systems and services on the basis of domestic law or pursuant to contract with a health professional and subject to the conditions and safeguards referred to in paragraph 3; processing is necessary for reasons

420. Article 90 omitted (31.12.2020) by virtue of The Data Protection, Privacy and Electronic Communications (Amendments etc) (EU Exit) Regulations 2019 (S.I. 2019/419), reg. 1(2), Sch. 1 para. 70 (with reg. 5, Sch. 1 para. 80); 2020 c. 1, Sch. 5 para. 1(1).
421. Words in Art. 9(2)(h) substituted (31.12.2020) by The Data Protection, Privacy and Electronic Communications (Amendments etc) (EU Exit) Regulations 2019 (S.I. 2019/419), reg. 1(2), Sch. 1 para. 9(5) and (6) (with reg. 5); 2020 c. 1, Sch. 5 para. 1(1).

of public interest in the area of public health, such as protecting against serious cross-border threats to health or ensuring high standards of quality and safety of health care and of medicinal products or medical devices, on the basis of domestic law which provides for suitable and specific measures to safeguard the rights and freedoms of the data subject, in particular professional secrecy.

224. Schedule 1 Part 1 of the DPA 2018 permits processing for 'health and social care purposes' (e.g., preventive or occupational medicine, the assessment of the working capacity of an employee, medical diagnosis, the provision of health care or treatment, or the provision of social care) and public health.

225. Section 11(1) of the DPA 2018 makes clear that processing for health or social care purposes etc.) will be subject to the conditions and safeguards referred to in Article 9(3) of the UK GDPR (obligation of secrecy). The circumstances in which an obligation of secrecy arises include processing undertaken by or under the responsibility of a health professional or a social work professional, or by another person who in the circumstances owes a duty of confidentiality under an enactment or rule of law. Section 195 of the DPA 2018 defines the persons who are regarded as 'health professional' and 'social work professional'.

226. The obligations of secrecy in public health will only arise if it is 'necessary for reasons of public interest in the area of public health'. Article 9(2)(i) of the UK GDPR requires 'suitable and specific measures to safeguard the rights and freedoms of the data subject, in particular professional secrecy'.

227. In both situations, no further example is provided with regard to the scope and nature of the obligation of secrecy, and presumably the common law and the professional standards of confidentiality will be applicable. The safeguard for professional secrecy simply repeats the formulation in section 11(1) (i.e., that processing must be under the responsibility of a health or social work professional or another person who owes a duty of confidentiality). The Department of Health and Social Care has also produced guidance and codes of practice relevant to the obligations of secrecy, such as records management.[422] In addition to complying with the lawful and fair processing provisions under the data protection regimes, within the National Health Service (NHS), the Caldicott principles will have to be considered. The Caldicott principles define the responsibilities with regard to the use of confidential information within health and social care organisations and sharing of data. The eight Caldicott principles are as follows:[423]

Principle 1: Justify the purpose(s) for using confidential information.
Principle 2: Use confidential information only when it is necessary.
Principle 3: Use the minimum necessary confidential information.

422. Records management code, available at: https://www.nhsx.nhs.uk/information-governance/guidance/records-management-code/.
423. *See* Department of Health and Social Care, The Caldicott Principles available at: https://www.gov.uk/government/publications/the-caldicott-principles.

Principle 4: Access to confidential information should be on a strict need-to-know basis.
Principle 5: Everyone with access to confidential information should be aware of their responsibilities.
Principle 6: Comply with the law.
Principle 7: The duty to share information for individual care is as important as the duty to protect patient confidentiality.
Principle 8: Inform patients and service users about how their confidential information is used.

§2. Legal Professional Privilege

228. There are two types of legal professional privilege (LPP): legal advice privilege and litigation privilege. The former protects communications between a legal professional and client that involve the giving or receipt of legal advice. The content of the communications will span their entire spectrum of legal advice. The latter is more narrow and relates to communications between lawyers or their clients and any third party that are reasonably seen as being connected to decisions with regard to anticipated or existing litigation.[424] According to the Information Commissioner, 'communications' will comprise 'a document that conveys information and it can take any form, including a letter, report, email, memo, photograph, note of a conversation or an audio or visual recording. It can also include draft documents prepared, e.g. with the intention of putting them before a legal adviser'.

229. In paragraph 19 of Schedule 2 DPA 2018, controllers are exempted from compliance with the listed information rights of data subjects such as Articles 13(4), 14(5)(d) and 15 of the UK GDPR and the first three principles of the Act (lawfulness and fairness, purpose limitation and data minimisation) where the data are subject to LPP) (or confidentiality of communications in legal proceedings, as this is known in Scotland).[425] The existence of LPP and the overriding duty of confidentiality to protect lawyer-client communications can engage data protection rules such as a subject access request (SAR). SARs are a useful litigation strategy design to unearth information relevant to proceedings. It is reasonably clear, in light of *Durant*, that the mere fact an individual's name is mentioned in a file that there will invariably be personal data for the purposes of data protection law.[426] The legal professional in this case (Taylor Wessing) was representing their client in an inheritance dispute. On receipt of the SAR, Taylor Wessing claimed that the SAR would entail in their expending considerable effort and time carrying out searches of their files to determine whether there was non-exempt material. The High Court[427] accepted the Taylor Wessing's claim, but this was rejected by the Court of Appeal

424. *See also* Legal Services Act 2007, s. 190.
425. *See Campbell v. UK* (1992) 15 EHRR 137, *Redbridge LBC v. Lee Johnson* [2011] EWHC 2861.
426. *Durant v. Financial Services Authority* [2004] FSR 573.
427. *Dawson-Damer v. Taylor Wessing LLP* [2015] EWHC 2366 (Ch).

on the grounds that data controller, when relying on LPP, still had to produce evidence showing that undertaking the search would result in disproportionate effort being expended.[428]

§3. Secrecy of Communications to the ICO

230. Article 54 of the EU GDPR which contained provisions dealing with obligations of professional secrecy which applied to supervisory authorities and staff has been omitted by the DPPEC regulations.[429] Sections 131 and 132 of the DPA 2018 mirror the obligations. Section 131 of the DPA 2018 provides that:

231. No enactment or rule of law prohibiting or restricting the disclosure of information precludes a person from providing the Commissioner with information necessary for the discharge of the Commissioner's functions.' The obligation of professional secrecy does not extend to the making of a disclosure which is prohibited by any of Parts 1 to 7 or Chapter 1 of Part 9 of the Investigatory Powers Act 2016. Section 132 (1) of the DPA 2018 aims to clarify the scope of the obligation of secrecy. It provides that the obligation of secrecy owed by the Information Commissioner, staff or agent, extends to information which:

(a) has been obtained by, or provided to, the Commissioner in the course of, or for the purposes of, the discharging of the Commissioner's functions;
(b) relates to an identified or identifiable individual or business; and
(c) is not available to the public from other sources at the time of the disclosure and has not previously been available to the public from other sources,
unless the disclosure is made with lawful authority.

232. A disclosure is deemed to be made with lawful authority only if and to the extent that:[430]

(a) the disclosure was made with the consent of the individual or of the person for the time being carrying on the business;
(b) the information was obtained or provided as described in subsection (1)(a) for the purpose of its being made available to the public (in whatever manner);
(c) the disclosure was made for the purposes of, and is necessary for, the discharge of one or more of the Commissioner's functions;
(e) the disclosure was made for the purposes of criminal or civil proceedings, however arising; or

428. *Dawson-Damer v. Taylor Wessing LLP* [2017] EWCA Civ 74, paras 57–85. *See also Guriev v. CSD (UK) Ltd* [2016] EWHC 643.
429. Article 54 omitted (31.12.2020) by virtue of The Data Protection, Privacy and Electronic Communications (Amendments etc) (EU Exit) Regulations 2019 (S.I. 2019/419), reg. 1(2), Sch. 1 para. 48 (with reg. 5, Sch. 1 para. 80); 2020 c. 1, Sch. 5 para. 1(1).
430. Section 132(2) of the DPA 2018.

(f) having regard to the rights, freedoms and legitimate interests of any person, the disclosure was necessary in the public interest.

233. The ICO is required by section 133(1) of the DPA 2018 to produce and publish guidance, particularly on the way privileged communications are received and handled.[431]

§4. Health, Social Work, Education and Child Abuse data

234. Schedule 3 DPA 2018 contains a number of exemptions designated as listed GDPR provisions.[432] These include social work, health, education and child abuse records. For example, a 'health professional' is exempted from complying with Article 15 of the UK GDPR, if its application to data concerning health 'would be likely to cause serious harm to the physical or mental health of the data subject or another individual'.[433] Part 4 Schedule 3 paragraphs 13–17 contains exemptions relating to education data. 'Education data' means personal data consisting of information which constitutes an educational record, but is not data concerning health.[434] Controlling access to the education data can, for example, be justified. For the purposes of this Part of this Schedule, the 'serious harm test' is met with respect to education data if the application of Article 15 of the UK GDPR to the data would be likely to cause serious harm to the physical or mental health of the data subject or another individual.[435] Paragraph 19 of this Schedule provides that Article 15(1) to (3) of the UK GDPR (confirmation of processing, access to data and safeguards for third country transfers) do not apply to education data to the extent that the serious harm test is met with respect to the data. Child abuse data is covered by Schedule 3, Part 5 of the DPA 2018. Child abuse will include physical injury (other than accidental injury) to, and physical and emotional neglect, ill-treatment and sexual abuse of, an individual aged under 18.[436] 'Child abuse data' is personal data consisting of information as to whether the data subject is or has been the subject of, or may be at risk of, child abuse.[437] As seen previously, the rights of access under Article 15 of the UK GDPR would not apply if it is not in the best interests of the data subject.[438] Other exemptions prohibited or restricted by an enactment will include human embryos, adoption records, special educational needs, parental orders and the role of the Principle Reporter.[439]

---

431. *See Proper Alliance Group Ltd v. The Royal Bank of Scotland plc* [2015] EWHC 1557 (Ch).
432. Schedule 3 Part 1 DPA 2018. Words in Sch. 3 para. 1 substituted (31.12.2020) by The Data Protection, Privacy and Electronic Communications (Amendments etc) (EU Exit) Regulations 2019 (S.I. 2019/419), reg. 1(2), Sch. 2 para. 93(4) (with reg. 5); 2020 c. 1, Sch. 5 para. 1(1).
433. Schedule 3 Part 2, para. 2(2) DPA 2018.
434. Schedule 3 Part 4, para. 17(1) DPA 2018.
435. Schedule 3 Part 4, para. 17(2) DPA 2018.
436. Schedule 3 Part 5, para. 21(4) DPA 2018.
437. Schedule 3 Part 5, para. 21(3) DPA 2018.
438. Schedule 3 Part 5, para. 21(2) DPA 2018.
439. *See* Sch. 4 and s. 186(1) of the DPA 2018.

Chapter 2. Churches and Religious Associations

235. There are no equivalent provisions in the UK data protection legislation to Article 91 of the EU GDPR. Article 91 has been omitted from the UK GDPR and there is no provision that recognises churches and religious associations as self-regulatory entities for the processing of personal data to the extent that they conform with the regulation.[440] Article 91(2) of the EU GDPR states that any rules developed by churches and religious associations must be subject to the supervision of an independent supervisory authority. There is also the additional requirement that the conditions laid down in Chapter VI of this regulation are complied with.

440. *See* Recital 165 EU GDPR and Art. 17 TFEU.

Chapter 3. Law Enforcement Agencies

236. The legal framework for the processing of personal data for law enforcement purposes is set out in Part 3 of the DPA 2018, which was enacted to implement the LED. It should be recalled that the Commission has adopted an adequacy decision on the basis of Article 36(3) of LED, finding that the data protection framework applicable to processing by UK criminal law enforcement authorities ensures a level of protection essentially equivalent to the one guaranteed by the LED.[441]

237. Part 3 of the DPA 2018 applies to the processing of personal data by competent authorities for the purposes of the prevention, investigation, detection or prosecution of criminal offences or the execution of criminal penalties, including the safeguarding against and the prevention of threats to public security.[442] Competent authorities include a person listed in Schedule 7 to the DPA 2018[443] as well as any other person to the extent that the person has statutory functions for any of the law enforcement purposes.[444] Intelligence services are not considered competent authorities and, therefore, do not fall under the provisions of Part 3 of the DPA 2018. The processing of personal data by intelligence services is regulated in Part 4 of the DPA 2018.[445]

238. Part 3 of the DPA 2018, which mirrors the LED, lays down six data protection principles in the context of law enforcement: (a) processing should be lawful and fair;[446] (b) the purposes of processing must be specified, explicit and legitimate;[447] (c) personal data must be adequate, relevant and not excessive;[448] (d) personal data must be accurate and kept up to date;[449] (e) personal data should be kept for no longer than is necessary;[450] and, (f) personal data must be processed in a secure manner.[451]

239. Similar to the LED, Part 3 of the DPA 2018 includes a number of data subject rights, including a right of information,[452] a right of access,[453] rectification,[454]

441. *See* above.
442. Section 31 of the DPA 2018.
443. Section 30(1)(a) of the DPA 2018. According to Sch. 7, competent authority is considered any United Kingdom government department other than a non-ministerial government department as well as the Scottish Ministers, any Northern Ireland department, the Welsh Ministers, chief officers of police and other policing bodies, other authorities with investigatory functions (such as Other authorities with investigatory functions the Commissioners for Her Majesty's Revenue and Customs), authorities with functions relating to offender management and other authorities (such as the Director of Public Prosecutions).
21 The Commissioners for Her Majesty's Revenue and Customs.
444. Section 30(1)(b) of the DPA 2018.
445. *See* below.
446. Section 35 of the DPA 2018.
447. Section 36 of the DPA 2018.
448. Section 37 of the DPA 2018.
449. Section 38 of the DPA 2018.
450. Section 39 of the DPA 2018.
451. Section 40 of the DPA 2018.
452. Section 44 of the DPA 2018.

erasure and restriction of processing,[455] as well as a right not to be subject to automated decision-making.[456] Furthermore, Part 3 of the DPA 2018 imposes several obligations on controllers – and where applicable to processors –, including to implement data protection by design and default,[457] to maintain records of all processing activities[458] to keep logs for a number of processing operations in automated processing systems,[459] to cooperate, on request, with the ICO[460] and to carry out impact assessments where the processing is likely to result in a high risk to the rights and freedoms of individuals.[461] Part 3 of the DPA 2018 also requires controllers and processors to implement appropriate technical and organisational measures to ensure a level of security appropriate to the risks arising from the processing of personal data.[462] Data breaches must be notified to the ICO[463] and communicated to the data subjects where the breach is likely to result in a high risk to the rights and freedoms of individuals.[464] Controllers are required to designate a DPO, unless the controller is a court, or other judicial authority, acting in its judicial capacity.[465]

240. Finally, Part 3 of the DPA 2018 contains specific provisions regarding international transfers of personal data for law enforcement purposes to third countries or international organisations.[466]

453. Section 45 of the DPA 2018.
454. Section 46 of the DPA 2018.
455. Section 47 of the DPA 2018.
456. Sections 49 and 50 of the DPA 2018.
457. Section 57 of the DPA 2018.
458. Section 61 of the DPA 2018.
459. Section 62 of the DPA 2018.
460. Section 63 of the DPA 2018.
461. Section 64 of the DPA 2018.
462. Section 66 of the DPA 2018.
463. Section 67 of the DPA 2018.
464. Section 68 of the DPA 2018.
465. Sections 69–71 of the DPA 2018.
466. Sections 73–76 of the DPA 2018.

Chapter 4. National Security Services

241. Personal data processing by 'intelligence services' or those processing data on their behalf is governed by Part 4 of the DPA 2018. This framework is separate from the general data processing regime (UK GDPR) and the law enforcement processing regime (Part 3).[467] Part 4 of the DPA 2018 has been drafted to ensure consistency with the Council of Europe Convention 108+.[468]

242. Part 4 applies to three specific services in the UK, collectively referred to as 'intelligence services': the Security Service, the Secret Intelligence Service, and the Government Communications Headquarters.[469] A controller is the intelligence service that determines the purposes and means of the processing of personal data.[470]

243. Part 4 sets out six data protection principles:[471] lawful, fair and transparent processing;[472] purpose limitation;[473] adequate, relevant and not excessive data;[474] accuracy;[475] storage limitation; [476] and data security.[477] Part 4 of the DPA 2018 provides data subjects with a right to information,[478] a right of access,[479] rights in relation to automated processing,[480] a right to information about decision-making,[481] a right to object to processing,[482] and rights to rectification and erasure.[483] Under Part 4, controllers can charge a fee for dealing with a subject access request.

244. Section 110 of the DPA 2018 provides for an exemption from a number of provisions in Part 4 of the DPA 2018 if this 'is required for the purpose of safeguarding national security'. If the exemption applies, it can exempt controllers from: the data protection principles (except the lawfulness requirement); the data subject rights; reporting of some personal data breach; and some of the powers of the Commissioner. National security is not defined, and according to the ICO guidance it 'can be interpreted in a flexible way to adapt to changing threats … It is generally understood to cover the security and well-being of the UK as a whole, its population, and its institutions and system of government. For example, it can

467. *See* ICO, Guide to Intelligence Services Processing https://ico.org.uk/for-organisations/guide-to-data-protection/intelligence-services-processing/.
468. *Ibid.*
469. Section 82(2) of the DPA 2018.
470. Section 83 of the DPA 2018.
471. Section 85 of the DPA 2018.
472. Section 86 of the DPA 2018.
473. Section 87 of the DPA 2018.
474. Section 88 of the DPA 2018.
475. Section 89 of the DPA 2018.
476. Section 90 of the DPA 2018.
477. Section 91 of the DPA 2018.
478. Section 93 of the DPA 2018.
479. Sections 94 and 95 of the DPA 2018.
480. Sections 96 and 97 of the DPA 2018.
481. Section 98 of the DPA 2018.
482. Section 99 of the DPA 2018.
483. Section 100 of the DPA 2018.

cover: protection against specific threats, such as from terrorists or hostile states; protection of potential targets even in the absence of specific threats; and international co-operation with other countries'.[484] The national security exemption is not blanket and should only be applied when it is necessary and on a case-by-case basis.[485] While direct or immediate harm or threat is not required for the exemption to be applied, 'a real possibility of an adverse effect on protecting national security in a broader sense'[486] must be shown. Controllers remain subject to the oversight of the ICO as to whether or not the exemption was used appropriately.[487] According to the DPA 2018, a Minister of the Crown can issue a certificate which is conclusive evidence that the exemption is required for the purpose for safeguarding national security.[488] Certificates may have a prospective effect, this means that they do not have to be in place before claiming the exemption.[489] The certificate may identify the personal data to which it applies by means of a general description.[490] The ICO publishes the existence of the certificates, and basic details about the certificate including the name of the Minister who signed it and the date of signing, together with the text of the certificate where possible (although this may be redacted in certain cases).[491] Any person directly affected by the issuing of a certificate may appeal to the Upper Tribunal against the certificate.[492]

484. *See above* ICO, Guide to Intelligence Services Processing.
485. *Ibid.*
486. *Ibid.*
487. *See* Memorandum of Understanding, ICO and the UK Intelligence Community https://ico.org.uk/media/about-the-ico/mou/2617438/uk-intelligence-community-ico-mou.pdf.
488. Section 111 of the DPA 2018.
489. *See above* ICO, Guide to Intelligence Services Processing.
490. Section 111(2) of the DPA 2018.
491. Section 130 of the DPA 2018.
492. Section 111(3) of the DPA 2018.

Chapter 5. Other Specific Regimes

245. The ICO has issued guidance on several other processing instances and regimes, including political campaigning practices and data analytics,[493] charity fundraising practices,[494] credit reference agencies,[495] individual electoral registration[496] and schools, universities and colleges.[497]

493. Political campaigning practices: data analytics https://ico.org.uk/your-data-matters/be-data-aware/political-campaigning-practices-data-analytics/.
494. Charity fundraising practices https://ico.org.uk/your-data-matters/charity-fundraising-practices/.
495. Credit https://ico.org.uk/your-data-matters/credit/.
496. Electoral register https://ico.org.uk/your-data-matters/electoral-register/.
497. Schools, universities and colleges https://ico.org.uk/your-data-matters/schools/.

Selected Bibliography

Academic Literature

Bamberger, K. and Mulligan, D., *Privacy on the Ground, Driving Corporate Behaviour in the United States and Europe,* 6 and 12 (MIT Press 2015).

Bennett, C. and Raab, C. *The Governance of Privacy: Policy Instruments in Global Perspective,* 68 (MIT Press 2006).

Christakis, T., '21 Thoughts and Questions about the UK/US CLOUD Act Agreement (and an Explanation of How it Works – with Charts)', (13 October 2019). European Law Blog, Available at SSRN: https://ssrn.com/abstract=3469704

De Hert, P. and Papakonstantinou, V *The rich UK contribution to the field of EU data protection: Let's not go for 'third country' status after Brexit*, 33 Computer Law & Security Review 354 (2017).

De Terwangne, C., 'Article 5. Principles relating to processing of personal data' 309, Kuner et al. (eds.) *The EU General Data Protection Regulation (GDPR)- A Commentary* (OUP 2020).

Kim, E., 'U.S.-UK Executive Agreement: Case Study of Incidental Collection of Data under the CLOUD Act' (2020) 15 *Wash J L Tech & Arts* 247.

Leveson, *An Inquiry into the Culture, Practices and Ethics of the Press,* 999 (London 2012).

Lloyd, I., *Information Technology Law*, 38 (Second edition, Oxford University Press 2004).

Lynskey, O., 'Courts, privacy and data protection in the UK: Why two wrongs don't make a right' (Maja Brkan and Enangelia Psychogiopoulou eds. Courts, Privacy and Data Protection in the Digital Environment, Edward Elgar 2017) 216.

O'Cinneide, C., *Human rights and the UK constitution* (British Academy Policy Centre 2012).

Rosemary Jay, *Data Protection Law and Practice* 2 (Sweet & Maxwell 5th Ed. 2020)

Tzanou, M. and Karyda, S., 'Privacy International and Quadrature du Net: One Step Forward Two Steps Back in the Data Retention Saga?' *European Public Law* 28 (1), (2022).

Selected Bibliography

Table of Cases

UK Courts

Court of Justice of the EU (CJEU)

European Court of Human Rights

Reports

Younger K, *Report of the Committee on privacy*, Cmnd. 5012, Her Majesty's Stationery Office, London 1972., 12
Lindop, *Report of the Committee on Data Protection,* cmnd.7341, 1978., 13
European Data Protection Supervisor, 'Opinion 6/2017 EDPS Opinion on the Proposal for a Regulation on Privacy and Electronic Communications (ePrivacy Regulation)' (24 April 2017)., 21
Law Society, response to the Ministry of Justice 'Human Rights Act reform: A Modern Bill of Rights' consultation (March 2022), (3 June, 2022), https://www.lawsociety.org.uk/campaigns/consultation-responses/human-rights-act-reform-a-modern-bill-of-rights-consultation-law-society-response., 24
Information Commissioner's Office, Notification of PECR Security Breaches (version 2.2), 25 May 2022, https://ico.org.uk/for-organisations/guide-to-pecr/communications-networks-and-services/security-breaches/., 27
Information Commissioner's Office, *Guide to Binding Corporate Rules (n.d),* https://ico.org.uk/for-organisations/binding-corporate-rules/., 60
Information Commissioner's Office, *Guide to the General Data Protection Regulation* (GDPR), 2018., 63
Information Commissioner's Office's guidance on the national security and defence exception, available at the following link https://ico.org.uk/for-organisations/guide-to-data-protection/guide-to-the-general-data-protection-regulation-gdpr/national-security-and-defence/., 64
Information Commissioner's Office's SAR Guide https://ico.org.uk/media/for-organisations/documents/2619803/right-of-access-1-0-20210520.pdf., 87
Information Commissioner's Office, *Guide automated decision making and profiling (n.d.),*https://ico.org.uk/for-organisations/guide-to-data-protection/guide-to-the-general-data-protection-regulation-gdpr/automated-decision-making-and-profiling/., 99
Information Commissioner's Office, *Big Data and Data Protection and Big Data, Artificial Intelligence, machine learning and data* protection (n.d.), https://ico.org.uk/media/for-organisations/documents/2013559/big-data-ai-ml-and-data-protection.pdf., 99
Information Commissioner's Office, *AI and Data Protection Risk Toolkit v1.0 (n.d.),*https://ico.org.uk/for-organisations/guide-to-data-protection/key-dp-themes/guidance-on-ai-and-data-protection/ai-and-data-protection-risk-toolkit/., 103
European Data Protection Supervisor, *Guidelines on the concepts of controller, processor and joint controllership under Regulation (EU) 2018/1725*, 9 November 2019), https://edps.europa.eu/data-protection/our-work/publications/guidelines/concepts-controller-processor-and-joint_en., 112
Information Commissioner's Office, Contracts and liabilities between controllers and processors https://ico.org.uk/for-organisations/guide-to-data-protection/guide-to-the-general-data-protection-regulation-gdpr/contracts-and-liabilities-between-controllers-and-processors-multi/, 118

Others

Table of Legislation

UK Legislation

EU Legislation

Index

The numbers here refer to paragraph numbers.

Index